PROVE THYSELF a man

Encouraging Your Son to Become
a Man of Character

CLAY ANTHONY & ANDY GOWINS

PUBLISHED BY COLD TREE PRESS
NASHVILLE, TENNESSEE

Visit us online: www.provethyselfaman.com

Scripture taken from the HOLY BIBLE, NEW INTERNATIONAL VERSION,
Copyright © 1973, 1978, 1984 International Bible Society.
Used by permission of Zondervan Bible Publishers.

Library of Congress Control Number: 2008923994

Published by Cold Tree Press
Nashville, Tennessee
www.coldtreepress.com

Printed in the United States of America
ISBN-13: 978-1-58385-253-8
ISBN-10: 1-58385-253-0

TABLE OF CONTENTS

INTRODUCTION: *Prove Thyself a Man* vii

ONE • *Be Strong and Courageous!* 1

TWO • *Keep the Charge—Be Holy.* 25

THREE • *Walk in His Ways—*
Be a Disciplined Man of Character. 47

FOUR • *Keep His Commandments—*
God Honors Obedience 85

FIVE • *How Will You Define Success?* 137

SIX • *Be Careful of How You Walk* 189

SEVEN • *A Father's Proverbs* 203

CONCLUSION: *He's Been Watching You* 215

Clay's boys at a T-ball game

INTRODUCTION

Prove Thyself a Man!

I n the off-Broadway production of *The Lion King,* there is a haunting scene that sets the tone of this work. Simba, the maturing cub and heir apparent to the throne, has run away from Pride Rock (home) and the responsibility of leadership that is uniquely his. At some point in his maturing youthfulness, he is confronted by friends and acquaintances from his past—Nala and Rafiki—which triggers a vision of his father, Mufasa, the dead lion king. "You are my son! You have forgotten who you are," the vision of Mufasa declares.

"Your father still lives!" Rafiki announces to a shocked and confused Simba.

"Really, where is he?" Simba asks.

Taking his staff, Rafiki strikes the puddle of water that Simba is gazing into and pointedly states, "He lives in you!" The scene ends with Simba gazing into the water at his own reflection, contemplating those words, "Your father still lives. He lives in you!"

Dads, our sons are the summation of who we are. It is true. Your boy is your son and you will live on in him. How many times have you caught yourself acting like your father; saying the same things he said; behaving the same way he behaved; liking or disliking the same things he liked or disliked? What kind of son are you training up? What kind of example are you setting for him to follow?

You have heard the old adage, "If mom isn't happy, nobody is happy." Well, here is another one for you, one that you might not have thought of. *"If daddy isn't holy, then nobody is holy."* Husbands and fathers whether you like it, understand it, ignore it or run from it, you are the recognized spiritual leader of your home and you are leading them somewhere. If your young children are not maturing in the faith, or your grown children are not mature in the faith, or if your wife is weak in her knowledge and practice of all things Godly, then it is up to you to do something about it. The responsibility itself is both trying and rewarding. One day you will be called before the King of kings and the Lord of lords, Christ Jesus himself, and you will be asked to give an account for the job, the task, He has given you. Be prepared because so far excuses have not settled so well with God.

Being a husband and a father is a full-time job. At no point are you off the clock. Your children are always watching you, especially your son. He is always watching, always listening, and always learning how to be a man, and that based upon your every move and action. What do you want him to see? What do you want him to take with him as he leaves home? What traits do you want him to exhibit when he begins courting a young lady? When he is your age and he is no longer under the authority of your leadership, what kind of man do you want him to be?

Think about this for a moment. What does a driver's license or a hunting license allow you to do? What do they say about your ability to do that activity? The answer is obvious; they act as a stamp of approval. A driver's license allows you to drive; a hunting license allows you to hunt; but do either of these acknowledge your ability to perform the task? At what point do our sons receive their license to be a man? Is there a rite of passage between fathers and sons that says to them, "Today, I have entered into manhood; now I am a man?" Is there a goal or an event that a young man can work toward that when he reaches it or achieves it, he will know that he has arrived at manhood? Is it when he graduates high school or college? What if he never graduates? Is it when he gets married? Some get married early in life and some, like Jesus, never get married. Is it when he loses his virginity? What if he is not married? That is not good. So when is it?

As you wrestle with this dilemma, as you rack your brain trying to arrive at an answer, rest assured that there is no set timetable for your son to become a man. That is an alarming fact. The dirty little secret that most of us dads want to ignore is that we are the problem. We want to tell our sons what to do, but we do not want to set the example of how a Godly, righteous man looks and acts.

THE PROBLEM

Here is the problem—everyone is going to follow something, whether it is satisfying the palate at their favorite restaurant or by pledging their undying support to their favorite sports team. Everyone is going to follow something. We are certainly not attempting to be party-poopers nor are we trying to rain on anybody's parade. No person reading this book could enjoy eating out more than we do; nor could anyone be a more avid sports fan than we. The problem with "followship," however, stems from the fact that while we are trying our dead-level best to raise our boys in the nurture and fellowship of Jesus Christ, we are confused at times as to who we are to be following. With all that could be written about the evils and trials facing today's family, let us be very honest and say upfront that this task is hair-raising, terrifying, and sidesplitting all at once. Simply stated, there are just too many options for our sons to follow as they grow up. To turn out a young man of eighteen or nineteen years of age that has the wherewithal to be a committed follower of the ways and means of Jesus Christ in today's culture would seem like an impossible mission.

So then, do we, as committed followers of Jesus, raise the white flag in surrender before we have even attempted the task? Do we, as committed husbands and fathers, resign our post at the first hint of trouble that would befall our sons, our families? Or do we establish a plan—a plan to pass our faith on to our sons, a plan that will ensure that they are walking in all the ways of the Lord? If there is no plan by which to point our sons to the Savior, then have we not in some major way already handicapped their ability to follow the Christ that we claim to follow? Will they then not be "unrestrained" in their ways—doing whatever is right in their own eyes? Do you see the problem now?

This book is the product of two fathers who desperately desire to instill in their boys a healthy fear of God, so that they might have wisdom and be restrained in their ways. The book you hold in your hands is our attempt to articulate to our sons what it means to be a Godly man. It is our attempt to establish a marker by which our boys can measure their success or their failure in striving after manhood. What you hold in your hands is truly a love letter that we (Clay and Andy) have composed for our sons. The plan that we laid out as we began this work was simple. We wanted to put down on paper our hopes, our dreams, and our words of advice for our boys—two fathers writing to three boys, sharing with them the advice and words of wisdom that we desire for them to have. We have written this work of love as if we were talking one-on-one to our sons—at times addressing them each individually, at other times talking to all three. Sometimes we address them from the perspective of one dad or the other, sometimes from the perspective of both. There will even be moments in this work when we step aside and talk candidly to the dads. To be honest with you, we have broken just about every convention of the English language when it comes to writing, and we have done so without apology. We have done all of this in the effort to equip our boys for the most important task of their lives—the pursuit of real manhood, which is the pursuit of Godly living. We have written this letter as if it were a last will and testimony to be given to our pre-adult sons in the event of our deaths; we have written simply to articulate a conversation that we hope to have one day with our "little men." This book is a conversation, a conversation that has began between our sons and us concerning manhood—a conversation that we invite you to share with us.

This conversation actually began before we even became dads. We would sit around with our wives and talk about the children we would someday have. Someday we would have a big Christmas tree with all the trimmings. Someday we would go to T-ball games and the beach. Someday we would order class rings and send birthday invitations. Before we knew it someday was upon us. In the middle of all of our "someday" conversations, however, the topic of religious beliefs never came up. Not once did we stress over the importance of church attendance or the role that the Bible would play in the raising of our children. It was not a point of discussion; we simply assumed that Christ would be the central focus of our family life. What else would we build our families' future upon? While we had no idea what it meant to bring a child home from the hospital or how to keep them safe and sound, there was one thing we were certain of— the heritage of our faith would not die with us. The heritage of our faith would be passed down to our children.

That brings us to this moment. A moment which finds both Andy and I sitting at our computers attempting to put into words the wisdom that we as young and nervous fathers have found in the beautiful plan that is God's Word. It is a plan for instilling the Christian faith into the lives of our sons. This wisdom that we have discovered cannot be found in a how-to manual. No child comes with a set of one-size-fits-all instructions. What works for our sons may or may not work in the lives of your children. Neither is this a work of pop psychology that will help you to dialogue with your children, nor will it tell you why your little ones are different from other children.

This conversation has been going on now for a little over seven years. At times it gets a little crowded with all the other "noise" in our lives. Sometimes the conversation is non-verbal in that our sons are simply watching their parents act and react to what life throws at them. Sometimes the conversation turns sour and sad, and at other times it sounds like rejoicing. One thing is for certain—this conversation is a non-stop attempt to invade the hearts and minds of our children to show them that God has called them to a higher definition of manhood than what they may see around them.

THE DEFINITION

The conversation that we have begun with our sons, even at their young ages, centers on the definition of manhood that God has placed in His Word. Yes, God did create man, and He left him with instructions for daily living. Throughout this book you will note that the authors hold to a very high view and respect for the Bible as God's final and authoritative word to humanity. Any conversation or definition that we might have with our children about life begins and ends with a copy of the Bible in our hands.

Turning to the Bible we find an immense number of examples of good and bad, righteous and evil men. Every man mentioned in Scripture, except for One, had his flaws. Many were brave, many were righteous, and many possessed wonderful qualities that our sons would be wise to emulate. For our definition, however, we have not chosen the example of a person but rather a set of qualities upon which to focus. These qualities are rather quite simple and can each be found rooted in the biblical text: discipline, gentleness, generosity, and faithfulness. These four little words have come to mean so much in our lives as young fathers.

It is the essence of these traits that we pray our sons will one day grow to practice. We invite you to eavesdrop on this conversation with our boys—a conversation that directs our sons to be men who are disciplined, men who are gentle, men who are generous, and men who are faithful.

Many of the thoughts expressed here are not original to us, and we will do our best to give credit where credit is due, for there is much wisdom in the counsel of Godly men. The journey into manhood that we present here is not a step-by-step process that we are trying to lead our sons to follow, but rather it is more of a lifestyle by which to live. Throughout the rest of their lives, there will be innumerable opportunities for our sons to show themselves to be men. It is our hope to adjust their focus and protect their hearts as best we can. It is our hope that they may be prepared to mature in their manhood and to ensure that their display of manliness is always undeniable and biblical. We are very proud of our sons and we would like to take a moment to introduce them to you.

CLAY'S SONS

So that you, the reader, can feel a little bit of ownership in the words that we are writing, I would like to introduce you to my two sons. First is Aslan Clayton. He was born while my wife and I were seminary students in Louisville, Kentucky. I will save you the "it was a dark and stormy night" bit, but please know that it was stormy and very late when this young man decided to grace us with his presence. His name was derived from one of my truest passions—literature. As a child, I grew to love each and every

CLAY ANTHONY & ANDY GOWINS

story of fantasy and adventure I could get my hands on. I distinctly remember being drawn to one particular character from a small book in the library at my elementary school. This character appeared in a series of novels for children, the first of which, that I read, was *A Horse and His Boy*.

In this story, a boy and his horse are running from a frightful sounding animal in the woods, only to discover that the frightful sounding animal was actually Aslan, the king of the woods, who was simply looking after the welfare of the horse and his boy. Aslan, the great lion king of the woods, reappears throughout the *Chronicles of Narnia*, a fantasy adventure series by C.S. Lewis. I remember reading in college that Lewis was once asked if Aslan was a type of Christ-like character. Lewis' reply was simple and has stuck in my mind ever since: "Aslan is not a type of Christ," Lewis said. "He is Christ."

Recently, the motion picture *The Lion, the Witch, and the Wardrobe* was released to the big screen. This has given my son many humorous chances to tell people that there was a movie made based on him. Even at his young age, my son has learned to master the fine art of being a good son. If I could sum his character up in one word, it would be joy. Rarely does this young man ever fail to bring joy into a room that he enters. Aslan has a rare case of joy each day. It is a joy that appears on his face as if every morning was Christmas morning.

This boy has a depth about him that I know he did not get from either of his parents. As you read on you will see the unique opportunity that being a part of our family presents Aslan to be a deep-hearted child. He cares deeply about every hurtful story that he hears and is quick to share his desire to do something. When Hurricane Katrina devastated the Gulf coastal region of our state, Aslan was quick to volunteer toys from his room and food from our pantry. Often he accompanies me on pastoral hospital visits and is quick to remind me to wash my hands and pray before I leave the room of any and all sick persons that we are blessed to visit. I truly enjoy my life with Aslan.

My second son is named Haddon Lanier. With an older brother named Aslan, any old common name would just not do. My personal theology and love for the work and the life of the Puritans drew me to the power and clarity of Charles Haddon Spurgeon. The man known as "The Prince of Preachers" brought great light and heat to the hearts of England during the latter part of the nineteenth century. The sermons and collective writings of this man left an indelible mark on my life and ministry. Understanding that Charles is a little on the common side of names and that Spurgeon would perhaps cause my youngest child problems in grade school, my wife and I agreed to name him Haddon. Lanier was the name of my father-in-law, who never lived to see Haddon born. My father-in-law was the first of our immediate family to pass away, and seeing that he left such a Godly legacy for my own children to follow, it made perfect sense to bestow his name upon his grandchild.

Haddon looks like a normal little boy, but Haddon is not normal. Haddon is sick, very sick. The technical name for his sickness is cystic fibrosis (CF). My wife and I have labeled it many other names at times. In a nutshell, Haddon has to have help breathing, eating, and digesting. How about that? Three of the simplest, most basic processes that I do every day—three fundamental practices that I have taken for granted my entire life—these three functions of living are killing my little boy. His lung function is hampered by the buildup of thick mucus in his lungs. While you and I are able to clear our throats and "expiate" what is congesting our bodies, Haddon cannot. He has to wear a specially designed vest twice a day that shakes his torso so as to loosen any irritations in his lungs. This keeps his lungs clean and healthy.

In addition to the vest, Haddon is required to take a fistful of medications each and every day. These medications help him to eat because his little pancreas does not want to function. At times it seems that his coughs are going to bring up sandpaper they are so dry. He takes other medications in order to keep his sinuses under control. He visits special nurses, dietitians, respiratory therapists, and doctors just to stay ahead of this monster that has attacked his body.

As bad as life with CF seems to anyone that reads about it, what really stinks about the entire situation is that there is no cure. In simple terms, CF is terminal. Just writing those words seems like I am sitting in an airport somewhere reading about some other little boy in a magazine that was left behind by someone on their way to Dallas or San Diego. It just does not seem possible that this little child that has a double-crowned head of hair like his grandfather and a personality that cannot be copied may have a life shortened by something in his DNA, something we cannot control. It is such a surreal situation.

How often have I replayed the scene that day in May of 2005, when I first heard that my son was sick! Did I hear the doctor correctly? Did he really say that there was "no cure"? Is that really my flesh and blood that is being held in an X-ray tube, by straps, crying for me? Is that really my voice that keeps saying, "Hold still, son; it will be just a little poke?" How can I reassure my sweet wife that all will be fine when I have read the same medical reports and Web sites that she has? Will I ever lose the sight of those huge tears that refused to fall; tears that filled the eyes of my oldest son as he asked me one Sunday morning prior to church, "Is Haddon really going to die?" Why is it that this little man who has a better church attendance and love for God than the majority of most good church folk three times his age has to face a monster that, barring a cure, will eventually take his life? I want you to read it from a father who has become an expert in such things: as far as I am concerned, Haddon is the bravest human being I have ever met.

Now keep in mind, CF is simply a diagnosis from a doctor. Our family is not limited nor are we defined by this disease. I have often told anyone that would listen that of all the families I know, there is not one that I would trade places with. Cystic fibrosis has been a very good thing for our family, thus far. I know that seems to be a very odd statement, but our family has proven it to be true. Remember how I described Aslan above? I cannot for the life of me remember a daily vest treatment that Aslan has not sat within arms reach of his little brother. I have heard Aslan say with a voice louder than the protests of his brother's, "Haddon, just do your vest! You have to!" Toys, television, and even supper have taken a back seat so that my firstborn can support his little brother through the trouble that has beset him. Aslan has a heart that is made for Godliness.

I have watched with such pain as Haddon not only has had to undergo treatments, but also the looks he gives when his pills are forgotten at home and the plans for dinner at the fast food restaurant have had to be abandoned. At more than one birthday party he has had to sit and wait for his pills well past the other partygoers diving into the cake and ice cream. Haddon has enough patience to calm his parents down when they have to kindly say things like, "I am sorry, he cannot have that without a pill," or "Do you have juice instead of milk?" I believe that I can state with confidence that every child that has ever lived has been known to whine, and Haddon is no exception. Yet, through everything that I have mentioned above, Haddon has never ever complained. The lungs that Haddon was born with are broken, but his spirit is far from being broken. He brings so much joy to my life.

Haddon's daily vest treatment

Andy's Son

Have you ever seen something with your eyes, experienced it with your senses, but refused to acknowledge its real and actual presence? That was my very first experience with my newborn son, Duncan. I can remember sitting to the left of my wife, holding her hand as the doctor pulled him from her womb (he was born cesarean), announcing that we were the proud parents of a baby boy. As the nurse placed him in my arms, I noticed that his left hand looked a little bit odd. You see, Duncan does not have a full grown set of fingers on his left hand. He is missing his pinkie finger, his ring finger, and his middle finger from the knuckle down. My eyes saw it, but my mind would not easily acknowledge it. This would not be the first surprise that Duncan would give us.

As he began to grow and mature, we noticed that Duncan was not going through some of the motor-skill categories that most normal infants and toddlers go through. One of the big red flags in his development was that Duncan never really crawled; he scooted on his rear or "one-arm-army-crawled" on his belly. Being the concerned parents that we were, we took Duncan to a specialist to be tested. This was when Duncan, my second-born, my one and only son was diagnosed with cerebral palsy.

Cerebral palsy is a disability resulting from a lack of oxygen to the brain before, during, or shortly after birth. It is outwardly manifested by muscular incoordination and/or speech disturbances. Unlike cystic fibrosis, cerebral palsy is not necessarily life threatening. We have no idea when Duncan could have been deprived of oxygen. He was born cesarean. There was no evidence of trauma to his umbilical cord, nor was there any report of trauma immediately following his birth. The only conclusion that we have come to is that his oxygen might have been interrupted for a short time early in my wife's pregnancy, at the same time his left-hand fingers were damaged. The condition that damaged his fingers is known as amniotic band syndrome. The best way to describe it is to liken it to a rubber band that is tightly placed over a body part and constricts or even prevents growth to occur. The affected area eventually separates from the body due to the constriction. Amniotic bands normally form over much larger appendages such as arms and legs, usually amputating that appendage. It is possible that Duncan suffered cerebral damage during this time.

Now lest you start weeping tears and feeling too sorry for our family and/or Duncan, let me share with you that he was diagnosed with a mild case of cerebral palsy; in fact, his mother and I would say a very mild case. As far as we can tell, his cerebral palsy has only manifested itself in his left leg and left arm. He has no control over the muscles in his left ankle; neither his ankle nor his foot bend or flex naturally. Because of his inability to flex his ankle, he is forced to wear an AFO (that is a fancy acronym for a brace). What does cerebral palsy look like? How does it affect him? Let me draw you a verbal picture. When he was six years old and in the first grade, Duncan played little league football. Nothing makes a father prouder (can you smell the testosterone?)—that is, until I had the chance to watch him play in his first game. Imagine the following scene. Duncan is lined up behind the quarterback in the fullback position. The snap count is barked and the football is hiked. The quarterback takes two steps backwards and pivots to his left, placing the pigskin squarely in Duncan's numbers. As my son grasps the ball and begins to run to the outside of the line, all that I can see is him running on his tip-toes, with his left arm drawn up against his body and his left hand dangling loosely at the wrist. Remember, Duncan's cerebral palsy affects the left side of his body. Because his left ankle and foot will not bend, he is forced to run on the tips of his left-foot toes. Hence, he has a natural tendency to run with a slight left favor. In other words, he does not run in a straight line. So there he is: my boy, running on his tip-toes, with his left arm drawn up into his body and his left hand dangling loosely at the wrist; running toward the left of the line, then toward the opposing team's bench, and then turning ever so slightly so that he is aimed at running toward the opposing team's goal. Luckily, he has a mild case of cerebral palsy. It did not manifest itself into his cognitive abilities. As he was running, he quickly realized that he was going in the wrong direction, corrected his course, and was able to carry the ball for a one yard gain. This is what a mild case of cerebral palsy looks like in the Gowins family.

All kidding aside, Duncan is one of the joys of my life. My wife and I praise God for Duncan's mild case of cerebral palsy every time we take him for a checkup at the Shriners Hospital. Our hearts are broken every visit as we see boys and girls who do not have mild cases of cerebral palsy. While Duncan is officially diagnosed with this physical handicap, he is not handicapped by any stretch of the definition. I share Duncan's cerebral palsy with you because it is an important part of the equation that has drawn Clay and his family together with my family. Whether it is a life-threatening disease or a handicap that threatens the quality of life that your child can expect to have, no father (or mother) wants his child to live like that. No father wants his child to experience an abnormal childhood devoid of simple pleasures; no father wants to see his child hurting or suffering. We are proud of our boys and we want them to grow into manhood, but more importantly, we desire that they experience the abundant life that Christ describes in John 10:10. We want them to drain every last vestige of joyful living from the "cup of abundant life."

Like Haddon, Duncan is not defined by his condition. In fact, most people do not even realize that there is anything wrong with him. What most people see is a blond-haired, blue-eyed boy who is full of life. Duncan is not defined by his condition; he defines his condition. As far as he is concerned, life is just one huge party and not only is he the guest of honor at this party, he is the party's main attraction. Since the day he was born, he has been a prankster; everything is a game. Now this might sound fun, but it can be a real challenge for a time-challenged, stress-filled parent. For example, how would you handle a young boy of seven who knows the household rule, "No throwing the football in the kitchen," but decides to question the boundaries of what exactly is the kitchen, or exactly what is "a throw," or does the rule also apply to basketballs, bouncy balls, and/or his spongy balls? Or what about his obsession with just one more question? I cannot count the number of times he has asked me not just one question about a topic we have just discussed, but like a gangster's "Tommy-gun," he spits out question after question—sometimes asking the next question before the last question has been answered. Many times, Duncan will ask the same question over and over again and no matter what answer you give him, he continues to ask and ask and ask. There are days when I am ready to pull my already thinning hair straight out of my head. His questioning spirit has gotten so challenging that Duncan often starts a conversation with the statement, "Dad, I've got ten questions."

Not only is he the household prankster and domestic pest (according to his older sister), Duncan is also the ultimate optimist. He does not understand the word "can't" or the concept of failure. He believes in his heart that there is nothing that he cannot do or accomplish. Duncan is a "cup half-full" kind of guy. He is always up for the next challenge.

Duncan is also a young man with a heart that longs to follow God. Not too long ago, while I was sitting in my office at church, Duncan came up to my desk, climbed onto my lap, and said to me, "Dad, can we pray and ask God to help me to be better?" He went on to add, "I really do want to do what is right and obey you and Mom." Wow! Moments like that make up for all the questions, games, and rule-bending antics. Two weeks ago while we were in Sunday morning worship, as we were singing praises to God and preparing for the senior pastor to bring the Word of God, Duncan asked me to help him take sermon notes. "Dad," he whispered to me, "I don't know how to take notes. I just don't get it. Can you show me how?" Yes!

Duncan is a young man with a generous and giving heart. My wife and I take turns praying with our children and to be honest, my wife gets to do this more often than I do; it seems that I have got too many meetings and ministry events that keep me away from home at bedtime. When I do kneel at Duncan's bedside for his bedtime prayers, I am amazed at the things for which he prays: non-Christian family members and friends, the terminally sick, children with cancer or other life-threatening diseases, often by name. In fact, I have even heard him pray for Haddon, whom he has only met once or twice. In spite of all of his frivolity and mischief, Duncan has a tender heart and he is very empathetic towards those who are hurting. Not only is he sensitive to give of himself in prayer for others, he is also very generous in serving and giving of his meager resources.

Every year during the Christmas season, our church has a special candlelight service that is dedicated to missions. At this service, everyone in attendance gets a candle. We line the walls of the sanctuary, turn off the lights, and then light our candles. During the service we take up a special offering that goes directly to international missions. That night, Duncan dug deep into his piggy-bank and gave a very generous offering, and he did it biblically—with a cheerful heart. Furthermore, unbeknownst to either his mother or me, Duncan had asked the senior pastor if he could serve by handing out the candles. I tell you, nothing could make a father more proud of his eight-year-old son than to witness him giving freely and happily of "his" money, or to see him standing at the front of the church handing out little bitty candle stubs as if they were gold coins. He took his ministry to the church and his service to God very seriously that night; that makes a father proud.

Oh, I could go on and on and tell you numerous stories about

Duncan, but it is enough for me to say that I love him with all of my heart. I am so proud of the young man he is already turning out to be. Like Clay's desire for his boys, I long for Duncan to be a Godly man. I want to see him mature into a genuine follower of Jesus Christ, not just a good church-going man. I long for him to prove himself a man!

LET THE CONVERSATION BEGIN!

In 1 Kings 2:1-3, we see David, Israel's greatest king, upon his death bed; we see the hopes that he left for his son, Solomon, in the form of a legacy; we see this legacy spelled out in David's instruction to his son in the phrase "prove yourself a man." Before we look at these instructions, a word should first be said to those who are thinking, "Okay, Clay and Andy, none of this applies to me." You might be thinking, "My kids are grown; they are too old"—so was Solomon. You might be thinking, "It's too late," but remember that David was on his deathbed; it is never too late. You might be saying, "My kids are too young," but we ask you, when is the best time to put the seal in the wax? The answer is obvious—when the wax is still soft. It is never too early to start; start today. Ah, we hear what you are thinking; you think you have got the "stumper" excuse, "Andy, Clay, I don't have any sons; I have daughters." Can we ask you a very serious question? As your daughters grow into adulthood, into womanhood, what type of man do you want her to find and marry? What kind of man do you want her to have for a husband? Listen to the father of a daughter (Andy): "Every word of wisdom that we are sharing with our sons is also a description of the man I hope my daughter, my little princess, will set her heart upon." Dads, teach your daughters what commitment looks like, how a Godly man acts and behaves. As young fathers, this is our hope: that in future days, when our sons are out of our sight and out from under the guidance of our hand, that they will demonstrate to the watching world what a genuine God-following, God-fearing man looks like and acts like.

LIFE APPLICATION QUESTIONS:

1. We mention our definition of manhood that includes the qualities of discipline, gentleness, generosity, and faithfulness. Are there any qualities that you believe we missed? Which ones would you add in order to have a quality definition of manhood with which to raise your son?

2. Have you ever shared with your son the story behind his name? What, if any, is the significance behind the name he was given?

3. Can you name at least one trait in the life of your own father that you have tried to model?

HELPFUL HINT:

Show your son this book and let him know that you are reading through it and want to sit down with him and discuss its contents.

PROVE
THYSELF
a man

CHAPTER ONE

Be Strong and Courageous!

avid's charge to his son Solomon is quite striking, "Prove thyself a man!" It is not a call to simply grow-up and become a man. It is the hard edge of a challenge—"Prove it!" Do not just tell me that you are a man. Show me that you are a man. How excited and frightened Solomon must have been on that day. Soon he would have to stand on his own two feet; soon he would have to decide for himself; soon he would have to be the man that his father had been preparing him to be. The proving, the showing, the becoming would require strength. It would require courage.

Have you ever thought about it? Have you ever asked yourself the question, "When did I become a man? When did my father challenge me to prove it?" It was during spring break of my freshman year at college that my father threw down the gauntlets of manhood—challenging me to prove it. Having been away from home for the better part of eight months and being completely broke, I had no choice but to return home for the week. There would be no trip to Florida for me. I stayed as late as I possibly could on that rainy Friday afternoon. In fact, my faded olive green, 1976 Chevrolet Caprice Classic was the last vehicle in the parking lot. Since I could not afford to go off to the beach with my friends, I made it my personal mission to see each one of

1

them off and on their way. My mission was a success.

With the sun sinking low in the horizon, I lowered myself into my car and behind the wheel. Putting the keys into the ignition, I gave it a good clean twist only to be greeted by silence—nothing. Sitting in the middle of an empty parking lot, it dawned on me that the college had been officially closed for hours. There was not a soul in sight that could help me. There was only one thing that a young emancipated college man could do. It was time to call Mom and Dad. They would help me. Dad would know what to do. After a short walk down the street to find the nearest pay phone, I was finally able to call home. Relief flooded my soul as I heard my father's voice. "Dad, I really could use some help. My car won't start. I don't have any idea what's wrong with it, and the college is closed. I'm locked out of my dorm room; I'm hungry; and I'm tired. How long will it take for you or Mom to come up here and get me?"

After what seemed like an eternity, my father simply said, "Andy, I'm really sorry to hear that. I would love to drive up and help you, but your mother and I have made other plans tonight, and then I've got to go into work early tomorrow, so we won't be able to help you. I hope everything works out and that we see you soon. I love you son, but I've got to go." Click. In my journey to manhood, no other single event stands out so vividly to me as that dark, rainy night in a little telephone booth, when the click and silence of an empty telephone line challenged me to "prove" that I was a man. That night required strength. It demanded courage.

I would discover years later that after my dad had hung up

on me, he sat by the phone for the next five hours waiting to hear from me. My mother would share with me that hanging up and not coming to my rescue was one of the hardest decisions that my dad ever had to make. You see, my dad realized that if I was ever going to step up and take responsibility for being a man, then I would need a moment, a catalyst that would challenge me to "put my money where my mouth was." It was not enough that I thought I was a man; it was not enough that I claimed to be a man; being a man required action. It demanded that I accept responsibility for myself and that I started behaving and acting like a man. One's claims must be demonstrated by one's actions. "What use is it, my brothers, if someone says he has faith but has no works? Can that faith save him? Faith, if it has no works, is dead" (James 2:14, 17). In other words, the manner in which you live your life had better back up the claims you make about your life.

I tell you the truth. I love my dad for hanging up on me. I respect my father for refusing to come to my rescue. I am thankful for a dad who thought enough of me to challenge me to "prove myself a man!" Boys, hear our hearts. There is coming a day when you too will be called upon to prove yourself worthy to be called a man. A day, not too far away, is rushing toward you when you will have to decide whether or not you will accept personal responsibility for your actions and behaviors.

SEEK WISDOM

Aslan, Haddon, and Duncan, over the course of the next several pages we want to share with you an authenticated formula for proving yourself to be a man. In God's perfect Word, the Bible, you can discover this formula. The apostle Paul informs his young protégé, his spiritual son, "All Scripture is God-breathed and is useful for teaching, rebuking, correcting and training in righteousness, so that the man of God may be thoroughly equipped for every good work" (2 Timothy 3:16-17). Boys, you can have confidence in this formula for manhood. It is straight from God's Word.

In this age of information, knowledge is plentiful. There are many sources of knowledge that will seek to teach you, to rebuke you, to correct and train you, but not in righteousness. These sources of knowledge seek to indoctrinate you into the knowledge of this world. Boys, righteousness and wisdom are scarce. Wisdom is much more than the simple accumulation of knowledge. True wisdom is having a basic attitude that affects every aspect of your life. It is having a biblical, Christian worldview. A worldview is the set of beliefs that inform the most important decisions in your life; it is the set of beliefs by which you live your life. Your worldview should answer four basic questions:

- Where did we (humanity) come from?
- Who are we (humanity)?
- What has gone wrong with the world?
- What can we do to fix it?

Your worldview is the source of your knowledge, and the Bible tells us that the foundation of knowledge is to fear the Lord (Proverbs 1:7). Such fear is demonstrated by how you honor and respect God, by how you live in awe of his power, and by the extent of your obedience to His Word. Fearing the Lord and seeking God's wisdom is an effective strategy for right living. Right living demands moral application, and moral application is grounded in trusting God and His Word. It requires practical application—acting on God's direction in daily devotions. Seeking God's wisdom, moral application, and practical application result in right living. Effective living is experiencing what God does with your obedience. Boys, your faith in God should be the controlling principle for how you process all knowledge, your understanding of the world, your attitudes, and your actions. Trust in God, and He will make you truly wise.

The person who has wisdom is loving, faithful, trusts in the Lord, puts God first, turns away from evil, knows right from wrong, listens and learns, and does what is right. According to God's Word, those who are wise benefit from a long, prosperous life. They enjoy the favor of God and other people. The wise have a reputation for good judgment and are successful in life. They enjoy health and vitality. They may benefit from riches, honor, pleasure, and peace. God's wisdom provides protection for those who seek such knowledge.

Boys, one of our greatest responsibilities, privileges, and tasks of being fathers is to encourage you to become wise. While wisdom can be passed on from parents to children, from generation to generation, ultimate wisdom comes from God. As parents the best we can do is to urge you and guide you to turn to God (Proverbs 4:3-4). This is exactly what David sought to do with his son, Solomon. From an early age, David taught Solomon that seeking

God's wisdom was the most important choice he could make. Boys, let us take a look together at David's advice, his encouragement, and his charge to his son to seek wisdom.

King David

There is no greater example of failed family leadership than King David—the giant-slayer, the man after God's own heart, the hero of the Old Testament. Imagine being part of the King David family reunion—a reunion that included members that were tied to murder, adultery, rape, and incest. Whoa! And you thought your family was bad. This describes the line of King David. Every one of these horrible sins stemmed from David's failure as a dad.

He reigned for forty years as the greatest king that Israel had ever known, yet David was a miserable father. He reared a son who would eventually rape his own half-sister, David's daughter (2 Samuel 13:14). He would have to suffer the grief of having one son murder another son (2 Samuel 13:29). David's son Absalom even plotted a rebellion to overthrow dear old Dad (2 Samuel 15:13), taking his father's kingdom and even threatening his father's life (2 Samuel 16:11). David would even have to give the order to have a son killed because of his unrighteous actions and behaviors. Toward the final days of his life, David's son Adonijah would boast saying, "I will make myself king" (1 Kings 1:5), and began to gather support among David's counselors and began to act as if he was the King of Israel (1 Kings 1:9-10). It is interesting what the author of 1 Kings has to say concerning David's parenting skills, "Now his father, King David, had never

6

disciplined him at any time, even by asking, 'Why are you doing that?'" (1 Kings 1:6). On his deathbed, David attempts to do what is right by his son Solomon.

In the final moments of his life, David lays out a definition of manhood that he hopes Solomon will follow. David had failed with his other children, but now as an old man speaking to his grown son, the mighty king, who had proven to be a horrible father, was attempting to set things right. David knew that he was about to pass the kingdom on to his son, but more importantly David knew that the advice he was about to give would shape the legacy he was leaving for his son to follow.

DAD DAVID

Boys (and dads), place yourself in Solomon's sandals for a moment. Can you imagine what the following scene must have looked like? What it must have felt like? Your father, the king, the hero of the nation, is old and in his final days. He is frail and at times a little senile; he is often cold and his body shakes and tremors with the creeping certainty of age and the hint of death. Then late one evening, long after the sun has disappeared over the horizon, as the cold desert winds whip through the night, there is an insistent rapping at your chamber door. Opening the door, you discover the king's personal servant.

"My Lord Solomon," he mutters, as he bends forward in homage and respect, "the King requests your immediate attendance." Grabbing your cloak, you head out into the dark night. It takes you several minutes to walk to the other side of the royal palace to the King's chambers. As you enter into the King's bed chamber, you notice at a glance several dignitaries, priests, and servants standing in waiting. Your eyes are automatically drawn to the King. He is sitting in his bed, propped up by pillows. There is an urgent look upon his face, a determination that furrows his brow.

The King's servant motions for you to take your place at the right of the King's bed. Then, with a quivering but stern voice, with hands lifted up in tightly shaped fists, the King, your dad, looks you squarely in the eyes and says with all of his might:

> I am about to go the way of all the earth, he said. So be strong, show yourself a man, and observe what the Lord your God requires: Walk in his ways, and keep his decrees and commands, his laws and requirements, as written in the Law of Moses, so that you may prosper in all you do and wherever you go, and that the Lord may keep his promise to me: If your descendants watch how they live, and if they walk faithfully before me with all their heart and soul, you will never fail to have a man on the throne of Israel. (1 Kings 2:1-4)

David, who was about seventy years old, reigned as king of Israel from 1055-1015 BC. He had anointed his son Solomon king and had made lavish preparations for Solomon to reign in his place once he went "the way everyone on earth must someday go." According to 1 Kings 1, David had lost his vitality and was cold and uncomfortable in his old age. He had become quite feeble in his last days, allowing Adonijah, as the heir-apparent to the throne, to establish himself as king over Israel. Upon hearing Adonijah's bold move to become the next king of Israel, both Nathan and Bathsheba (Solomon's mother) moved quickly to convince David to take steps by which Solomon was re-anointed and proclaimed king over all Israel.

Following this, his final charge to his son, David died and Solomon reigned as king over Israel for forty years. The final words of a father to a son are always significant, especially when royal power and divine purposes are involved. As death drew near, David gave Solomon a personal charge, from father to son: Take courage and be a man. David knew that he had failed as a father, and his legacy as Israel's sovereign monarch was in jeopardy of failing as well. With failed relationships with nineteen sons by marriage, several others by concubines, and one daughter, Solomon was his last hope to set things right. David's charge to Solomon directs his son back to the truth of God's Word, to the directives of God's law, and to the covenantal promises of Deuteronomy proclaimed by God's servant Moses.

WARRIOR DAVID

For all of David's years as a monarch, as a refined and dignified sovereign, David was a soldier at heart. It should not surprise you that he began his charge with words that have the ring of a battlefield charge: Be strong; prove yourself a man. In fact, it reminds you of a line you would expect to hear in a movie such as *Braveheart* or *We Were Soldiers Once*. It is a challenge that moves you at the very core of your being: "Take courage and show the world this day that you are a man!" David's challenge is a "gut-check." What followed was of special importance; it was how Solomon would manifest strength and courage: Solomon would be strong and manly only as he ordered his life by God's commands. Wow, if only David would have had ears to hear his own words of advice, maybe then his fatherhood track record might have been better. The priority of Solomon's personal life and of his royal administration would have to be grounded in a commitment to pursuing and doing the will of God.

The king of Israel was not to be like the pagan kings; he was not a law unto himself. Israel's king was to be a man under orders, the orders of the true King of Israel—Yahweh. Therefore, the king must walk in such a way as to keep God's decrees and commandments as they were recorded in the Law of Moses. The use of these various terms (His ways, His decrees, His commands, His laws, and His requirements) simply reinforced the single most important task of the king: The king's responsibility to honor the ways and words of God (Deuteronomy 17:18-20). Solomon was to be faithful to follow and to keep the Word of God.

A man after God's own heart

The concept of biblical faithfulness means much more than simply maintaining a life that is conformed to God's standards; more importantly, it also means to have a heart that is committed to God. "Hear, O Israel! The Lord is our God, the Lord is one! You shall love the Lord your God with all your heart and with all your soul and with all your might. These words, which I am commanding you today shall be on your heart" (Deuteronomy 6:4-6).

Heart-directed and dedicated faithfulness (sold-out devotion) is essential to understanding the theology and theme of 1 Kings. Life's central battle is the battle for the heart.

- 1 Samuel 16:7—"The Lord does not look at the things man looks at. Man looks at the outward appearance, but the Lord looks at the heart."
- Psalm 51:10—"Create in me a pure heart, O God, and renew a steadfast spirit within me."
- Romans 8:27—"He who searches our hearts knows the mind of the Spirit, because the Spirit intercedes for the saints in accordance with God's will."
- Hebrews 4:12-13—"For the word of God is living and active. Sharper than any double-edged sword, it penetrates even to dividing soul and spirit, joints and marrow; it judges the thoughts and attitudes of the heart. Nothing in all creation is hidden from God's sight. Everything is uncovered and laid bare before the eyes of him to whom we must give account."

There is no substitute for maintaining a heart of faithfulness and a lifestyle of obedience. Biblical discipleship is all about the motives of the heart. It is about faithfulness. As you grow into adulthood and you face the challenge of becoming a man, we want you to hear the impassioned words of a father: "Be strong Son, and prove yourself a man!" Faithfulness is about becoming passionate for the glory, the honor, and the purpose of God. It is not about following the letter of the law, nor blindly committing to the "shalls" and "shall nots." Do not misunderstand us. We are to "walk in His ways and follow His commands" whether we want to or not—that is being a responsible follower of Christ. Such a lifestyle, however, is not the heart and soul of Christian faithfulness. Such a life is the stuff of law, the stuff of the Old Covenant, the stuff of Pharisees. What we are called to is loving obedience simply because we love Him who first loved us. Obey the Lord your God. Walk in His ways, not because you have to, but because it is the right thing to do—because He is worthy of your worship and obedience.

Last, but not least, there are consequences to living such a lifestyle. David reminded Solomon of God's promises. Solomon would have personal success if he would simply "Be strong and show himself to be a man." This concept of "prosper" contains the idea of acting with skill and insight, making right choices. The result of success would not be the accumulation of wealth, power, prestige, or stuff. The result would be that "He would be like a tree firmly planted by streams of water, which yields its fruit in its season. Its leaf does not wither; and in whatever he does, he prospers" (Psalm 1:3).

APPLICATION TO LIFE

Boys, pay close attention. From David's deathbed conversation with Solomon, we gather one little phrase that is the basis of our definition of manhood—"prove yourself a man." It literally means exist as a man; be the man. Boys, whenever the world looks at you they are to see the epitome of what a man looks like. When you speak, your words are to be spoken like a man. When you are courting your future wife, be certain that she knows she is marrying a man—a man who understands the concepts of commitment and honor. Wherever there is a need for accountability, courage, work, peace, or responsibility, that is where we want to find our sons. By the grace of God, if we are successful, this is the kind of men our sons will become. Boys, hear the hearts of your fathers. We want sons who are able to "prove themselves to be men"—men who will demonstrate to the entire world what three God-fearing disciples of the Lord Jesus Christ look like.

We want you to be men like Shadrach, Meshach, and Abednego who boldly told king Nebuchadnezzar, "We do not need to defend ourselves...the God we serve is able to save us...But even if He does not...we will not serve your gods or worship the image of gold" (Daniel 3:16-18). Men who take God seriously and obey His Word: "You shall have no other gods before me. You shall not make for yourself an idol...You shall not bow down to them or worship them; for I am a jealous God" (Deuteronomy 5:7-10). Men who can say, "The Lord is my light and my salvation—whom shall I fear? The Lord is the stronghold of my life—of whom shall I be afraid" (Psalm 27:1-2). Boys, we expect much from you and we know that much is expected of us. We know that you are counting on us to take leadership and to help you discover how to prove yourself to be a man.

WE WANT OUR SONS TO WALK IN HIS WAYS
The first part of 1 Kings 2:3 says, "Keep the charge of the Lord your God, to walk in His ways." This will be one of the most difficult challenges you will be faced with in life, but walking in

13

His ways is as easy as making the right choices in life. It is easy because it is simply making the right choice one decision at a time. The difficult part is making the right decisions. Boys, your task is to be obedient and follow God. Walking in His ways is a figure of speech. It implies that you are to imitate the very character and nature of God. To shy away from that which is ungodly; "Do not imitate what is evil but what is good, anyone who does what is good is from God" (3 John 1:11). The burden rests squarely upon our shoulders. It is all about our ability to protect you. If we are diligent, if we work hard enough, if we mind our Ps and Qs, then we can act as a shield against what seeks to hurt and destroy you. "The thief comes to steal, kill, and destroy" (John 10:10); and again, "The world has hated them, for they are not of the world any more than I am of this world" (John 17:14). By doing all that we can to train you up in righteousness, we can keep you on the right path—walking the way of Christ. "Train a child in the way they should go, and when he is old he will not turn from it" (Proverbs 22:6).

Boys, our job is to keep you focused upon the path of righteousness, on the way you should go. Do you know what mules and thoroughbreds have in common besides their tails? They only have one other thing in common; they both wear blinders when they are working. Do you know why? The blinders help to keep the distractions at bay. Whether it is plowing a field or running in the Kentucky Derby, if they were to get their eyes off the goal, that prize which has been set before them, then there is no telling which direction they would run or how straight the plant rows would be. This is why the apostle Paul would write "in a race all the runners run, but only one gets the prize. Run in such a way as to get the prize" (1 Corinthians 9:24-25).

By the grace of God, we will go to any lengths to protect our children and to encourage them to keep their eyes on the prize that has been set before them. There are those in the pop-psychology movement who would refer to such protection as sheltering. Is sheltering such a bad thing? On August 29, 2005, there was a whole lot of sheltering occurring along the Mississippi Gulf Coast as Hurricane Katrina made landfall. Loved ones went to great lengths to protect their families. If alcohol, drugs, bad grades, premarital sex, disrespectful attitudes, pornography, or any other unrighteous, evil act, or any behavior threatens one of our boys (or for that matter, Andy's little princess, his precious daughter), then you had better believe that we will be fighting for the very lives of our children. We want to leave behind sons that can be found walking in the ways that God has prescribed.

WE WANT OUR SONS TO KEEP HIS CUSTOMS

David continues on in 1 Kings 2:3 by describing the means and/or methods by which Solomon will be able to keep the charge to prove that he is a man. Manhood is not defined by age, status, or even by the accomplishment of some great feat. Manhood is defined as being obedient to the customs and manners established by God. It is the divine command "to be holy because I am holy" (1 Peter 1:16); it is David's admonition for his son to walk in His ways. How will Solomon be holy? How will he be able to walk in God's ways?

David tells him that he will only be able to be holy and walk in God's ways, if he commits to keeping God's statutes—God's customs and traditions. Boys, can you think of some of the traditions that you have celebrated? They may have been traditions or customs that occur in conjunction with a holiday (we always set up our Christmas tree the Saturday after Thanksgiving) or perhaps a birthday (a special birthday plate or birthday meal); regardless of when, what, or why the custom occurs, one thing is for certain—everyone has "some" customs or traditions they keep. Some customs either make no sense or we forget why we keep them. We often carry on family traditions not certain of their history or significance. Have you ever heard the statement, "Well, we've always done it that way"? We never want that to be the case when it comes to your Christian walk, the living out of your faith. We want you not only to know, but we want you to remember and remember often that there is a reason why we gather on Sundays (Hebrews 10:25) and "Keep the Sabbath day holy" (Exodus 20:10). We want you to remember that there is a reason why we believe that marriage is sacred between one man and one woman (Matthew 19:5; Genesis 2:18-25; Ephesians 5:31-32). Remember that there is a reason we support missions throughout the world with our resources (Matthew 9:37-38; 28:18-20); there is a reason why we protect the unborn (Genesis 1:26-27; Psalm 139:16). There is a reason why it breaks our hearts when people mention Darwin as fact (Genesis 1:1-31; Psalm 102:25; 89:11; 90:2).

Boys, in our households we know that there is a reason for all of these customs and many more not mentioned; that reason has a name—Jesus. God's Word informs us,

16

In the beginning was the Word, and the Word was with God, and the Word was God. He was with God in the beginning. Through him all things were made; without him nothing was made that has been made. In him was life, and that life was the light of men. The light shines in the darkness, but the darkness has not understood it. (John 1:1-5)

When you are asked to give an answer or an account for what you believe, you cannot simply say "Just because." I cannot speak for Clay, but I remember growing up and thinking "just because" must have been my mom and dad's favorite answer for everything. Boys, forgive us for the many times we have uttered such words. God, forgive us for missing a divinely appointed moment to teach our children about their Heavenly Father and Your wonderful creation. The apostle Peter gives a gentle reminder to all believers, "always be ready to make a defense to everyone who asks you to give an account for the hope that is in you, yet with gentleness and reverence" (1 Peter 3:15). There is a reason for your faith and a reason for you to practice your faith. We do not want you to grow up to be what we despise the most in life—a dumb, ignorant Christian. Listen to what Jesus has to say about such believers, "I know your deeds, that you are neither cold nor hot. I wish you were either one or the other! So, because you are lukewarm—neither hot nor cold—I am about to spit you out of my mouth" (Revelations 3:15-16). Boys, we give you this, our pledge—you will know what you believe and why you believe it.

WE WANT OUR SONS TO BE OBEDIENT TO HIS RULES

Take a careful look at the end of 1 Kings 2:3. Read the last part of David's charge to his son, "Keep the charge of the Lord your God, to keep His commandments." Do you understand how a biblical covenant works? Two parties meet and agree on the terms of a contract, which holds the two together. Do you realize that God made His covenants with mankind knowing full well that He was dealing with imperfect humans? Humanity has never made a promise that we could not wait to break. As we strive to pass the faith on to you, as you strive to live faithfully under the power of the promises that God has declared, we pray that you will strive to obey Him in all that you set your mind, your heart, and your hands to do.

There is a little motto that we think of often. It is a motto that we want you to tattoo to your souls: *obedience over excellence.* "For I delight in loyalty (obedience) rather than sacrifice, in knowing God rather than burnt offerings" (Hosea 6:6). What does God desire? The Lord your God desires and demands your heartfelt attention rather than your meaningless motions of duty. It is the biblical principle that God honors obedience. Now hear your fathers very carefully, boys. We want you to do all things excellently, doing them all for the glory of God. However, we never want you to be guilty of going through the excellent motions of worship because of duty or obligation. Obedience to God is not rooted in obligation, but rather it is birthed in loving God with all of your heart, mind, strength, and soul (Matthew 22:37). Remember, to obey Him is to love Him (John 14:15).

We want you to be excellent in all things, but first we want you to be obedient. Do we want sons who seek the spot light or who choose righteousness? Do we want sons whom everyone adores and likes or sons who have personal integrity? Do we want sons that are at the top of their professions or sons that are known for their honesty? Do we desire for our sons to have large houses in which to live or do we want our sons to have their houses in order?

Boys, obedience to God may cost you a promotion or an award. It may even get you arrested. Obedience to God's will in your life may take you overseas into a hostile mission field. It might call you to a life of singleness, as it called the great missionary Lottie Moon. It may even call you to become a martyr for the faith, "to take up your cross" and "to lay down your life" even as it did Jim Elliot (a missionary to South America). But, such obedience would make the hearts of these two fathers glad. Such obedience would make us proud to proclaim, *"That's my boy! He has proved himself to be a man!"*

Obedience to God will most certainly not make you popular here on earth, but your names will be known in heaven. The Lord knows who suffers in His name, and all of heaven gives honor to Christ's martyrs. Boys, we pray that you are found faithful before God, faithful in keeping your end of the covenant that you have made with God.

This day I call heaven and earth as witnesses against you that I have set before you life and death, blessings and curses. Now choose life, so that you and your children may live and that you may love the Lord your God, listen to his voice, and hold fast to him. For the Lord is your life. (Deuteronomy 30:19-20)

It is a delight to live this way. David delighted in the terms of the covenant that God had placed before him: "I shall delight myself in Your commandments, which I love" (Psalm 119:47).

WE WANT OUR SONS TO BE KNOWLEDGEABLE OF HIS PLANS

1 Kings 2:3 is packed with information on defining manhood. David's next words turn to following the plans of God throughout your life: "Keep the charge of the Lord your God, to keep His ordinances." An ordinance is an authoritative decree or direction. It is a law set forth by a governmental authority. It is a legal term used to describe "something" ordained or decreed by God. We have ordinances (laws) that we have to live by today, right?

Aslan and Haddon, while preaching one Sunday morning, your dad asked his congregation for a show of hands if they knew that driving barefoot was actually against the law. You would have been surprised at the number of smart, educated people who honestly believed that this was a law, an ordinance. That it was illegal to operate a motor vehicle while being barefoot. You should have seen the looks on their faces as he confessed that he had just invented this rule. It is not against the law to drive barefooted. This little example simply illustrates that some people are just ignorant of what is and is not a part of the law. Boys, do not be ignorant of God's law.

You should not have to wonder, "What does God want from me?" God has made His will known. It is not necessary for you to second-guess God's intention. He has made it very clear what He expects from those who would walk in His ways. We do not want our sons to go through life guessing what it is that God expects and requires of them. David must have instilled this same particular hope in his son. After David goes the way that everyone must go (death), Solomon had the opportunity to ask God for anything (1 Kings 3:5-14):

God: *Ask me for anything your heart desires.*
Solomon: *Give me wisdom.*
God: *You could have asked to be rich but since you asked for a good thing like wisdom, I will make you both wise and rich.*

God is faithful and true. We are told from Scripture that Solomon did indeed become the richest man in the then-known world; but more importantly, we are also told that people from around the world, the nations came to seek out Solomon's wisdom and his counsel. We want sons that know what is right and they know it so well that others seek them out for advice. We never, ever want the words "Uh, I dunno" to come from their lips, particularly when it comes to the ways of God.

WE WANT OUR SONS TO BE BEACONS

"Keep the charge of the Lord your God; keep His testimonies," David says to Solomon. Our three boys are four, seven, and eight.

At these ages our sons are really good at doing two things—identifying right and wrong actions, and the not-so-lost art of tattling. Boys, do you know the difference between a tattletale and a lighthouse? A tattletale tells you what someone else is doing (right or wrong), while a lighthouse warns you about what someone else has already done (right or wrong).

We want you to be lighthouses, beacons in the darkness. Do you know why you never see a lighthouse in Nebraska? The answer is obvious. There are no ships in Nebraska, because there are no shorelines in Nebraska. Lighthouses are located along the shoreline for a reason. At some point in history, some boat ran aground and foundered upon the rocks along the shore; boats ran aground so often that there was a need to put up a warning sign—a lighthouse. With no warning sign, with no beacon present to warn the people, the memory of shipwrecks would soon be forgotten and other boats could come crashing in.

Boys, we want you to have a discerning eye and a discerning spirit. It is good to be a little skeptical. "Dear friends, do not believe every spirit, but test the spirits to see whether or not they are from God" (1 John 4:1). Be a student of history; always have your eyes wide open to discern the actions of those around you. Whether it be in your family life, your church life, your work experience, or even in your observations of the government, be ready to act like a beacon. Be ready to encourage those who are doing right. A beacon can be used to identify the way. It can also be used to warn those who are not doing right. It can be used to identify dangers that should be avoided. The key is for you to always remember that your authority is the Word of God. Speak from God's Word, not your own opinion or preferences. Living like this will never get you interviewed by Oprah, but it will guard your soul against certain disaster.

King David called Solomon's attention back to the Law of Moses. He wanted Solomon to remember what God had clearly stated in the first five books of the Old Testament—the law. At no point did God give a loophole or an escape clause in His law. You are to keep His Word and act like a lighthouse, a beacon for the world to see. We want our sons to know God's Word better than they know their own reflection. In a world set against God and His ways, we want sons who will remember that now famous line from the sermons of Billy Graham, *"The Bible still says..."*

LIFE APPLICATION QUESTIONS:
CHAPTER 1

1) Do you have a scene in your memory bank like Andy and his car not starting that your dad used to inch you closer to manhood?
2) What part did God and His ways play in how you were raised?
3) Taking your answer from #2 above, what God-centered customs did you bring into fatherhood from your childhood?

HELPFUL HINT

Be it a holiday, birthday, or any other day of special recognition, revisit a custom from your childhood that you can share with your son. Better yet, begin a new custom of your own!

- Read the Nativity story out of the Bible during the Christmas season and have your child place figurines into a Nativity set as you read it.
- Give your child the chance to pick out his or her favorite restaurant and take the family there on their birthday.
- Write your son a letter to be opened on a special day such as graduation or perhaps his wedding day.

CHAPTER TWO

Keep the Charge—Be Holy

I T IS ALL ABOUT THE CHOICES
When I was eight years old, my dad taught me a life-lesson that I have never forgotten. It was an early spring day, unseasonably warm and fresh after a cold and snowy winter. We were out in dad's workshop cleaning up when suddenly he asked me if I wanted to go shoot my pellet gun. What red-blooded, American eight-year-old does not want to shoot his pellet gun? At my house, there was never any of that *Christmas Story,* "Ralphie, you'll put your eye out" anti-gun propaganda "junk" that seeks to neuter the machismo of anyone of the male persuasion—can I get a guttural grunting noise from all the Tim the Tool Man fans? Of course the answer was "Yes!"

As I was loading my pellet gun, a Christmas gift from four months earlier, my dad was setting up aluminum soda cans in our backyard. We took turns shooting, loading, and setting up cans for the next hour or so. It was a great afternoon, one of those days that goes down in your "best days" memory file. On our way back to dad's workshop, we saw a blue jay hopping around in the branches of the trees that shaded our driveway. "I bet you can't hit that bird," my father challenged me.

Carefully, I chambered a round into my new pellet gun. I raised the butt of the stock to my shoulder. Snugly I adjusted the fit and sighted down the barrel. Squeezing the trigger gently, I fired my pellet gun. Now this was before such cinematic movies as *The Matrix*, where for the first time (that I can remember) you were able to visually track the movement and motion of an object such as a bullet or a pellet; but I tell you honestly, I can remember watching the pellet fire from my gun, fly across the air, and penetrate the soft down of the blue jay's breast. The slow motion fall of that bird is etched in my mind. One moment the bird was chirping and singing as it hopped from branch to branch; the next moment it was lying on the gravel of our driveway—dead.

Excitedly, I ran over to where the blue jay had fallen and as I bent over to examine my handiwork, the reality of the situation dawned on me. This beautiful creature that God had created was dead. It would never sing again. It would never soar through the sky again. It would never see its family again. That blue jay was dead because I had killed it. Tears began to swell up in my eyes. I tried my hardest to hold them back because I did not want my dad to see me crying. After all, my dad was a great hunter. He hunted deer, duck, rabbit, and squirrel every year; he killed "things" all the time. I knew that he was planning on taking me hunting with him next year; what would he say if he saw me crying because of a stupid, silly blue jay?

Holding back a flood of tears, I felt my father's hand resting upon my shoulder. I raised my head to look at him, expecting to see a smile or a grin of approval, but when I looked into my father's face I saw tears trickling down his cheeks. That was more than I could bear; suddenly the dam that was holding back my tears burst and I began to sob uncontrollably.

On bended knee, with his arms tightly around me holding me tightly to his chest, my dad and I wept for what seemed like an eternity. Finally, he pushed me back an arm's length from him and looked me squarely in the eyes. "Andy," he started to say, "We've just killed something for no reason. We just killed that bird simply because we wanted to, for the pure simple joy of killing. Son, we don't kill for fun." He went on to talk to me that day about the responsibility of choices in the context of hunting. My dad instilled within me a deep sense for only killing that which I would consume, that which I would eat or use—to never simply hunt or kill an animal for fun. "Every time you aim your gun," he told me, "or pull your trigger, you have a choice to make."

Many years have passed by since I was eight. I have killed many an animal and I love to hunt. But I have never forgotten the lesson I learned that unseasonably warm spring day. Once you have made a decision, once you have acted on that decision, your actions cannot be changed or mended. When I pulled the trigger, my decision had been made. It could not be undone. There was no way to "undo" killing that blue jay. When a decision is made, it is what it is.

Boys, as we start this conversation we want you to understand this simple biblical principle: there are consequences for your actions and your decisions. A decision made is an action that cannot be undone. It may be rectified; it may be re-addressed; it may be reviewed; but it can never be undone. The Bible uses many different terms to describe the decision making process. One of those terms is the Greek word *krino*. It literally means "to separate, to distinguish, to select, or even to judge." Let us illustrate this for you through a quick object lesson.

Go get a piece of paper (yes, we really want you to go get a piece of paper). Now firmly grasp that piece of paper with both of your hands. Rip the paper down the middle (go ahead, do it). What do you have? The answer is obvious; this is not a trick. You have two pieces of paper. Now put those two pieces back together again, just like they were prior to ripping them. Okay? You can use glue, tape, staples, or whatever else you might want to try. Go on, put them back together, just like they were before you ripped them. Are they back together yet? What? What do you mean you cannot get them back together *just* like they were before you ripped them? You have got them taped together and they look pretty close to being just like they were, but you are right. Once you have ripped them, you will never be able to get them back just like they were.

That is the way it is with a decision. Once you have made the decision, it is made. It is as definite as if you had ripped a piece of paper in two. It cannot be re-decided. You will never be able to return to the "pre-decision" situation exactly as it was prior to the making of the decision; and do not forget, that with every decision you make, for every action that you take, there will be consequences—things that happen because of the decision you made. It really is all about the choices that you make—not just the big choices, but the little choices as well. Remember the apostle Paul's challenge, "Whatever you do, do it all for the glory of God" (1 Corinthians 10:31). Whatever decisions you make, whatever actions you take, whatever choices you determine, do them all for the glory of God. In doing so, you will never be sorry about the consequences of your choices—your decisions.

WHO WILL YOU FOLLOW?

As David called his son Solomon to his bedside, it is easy to imagine that David was worried about many things. As we have already pointed out, David was not a very good father. He was not very successful in the "daddy business." And, even though he was a man after God's own heart (Acts 13:22), David had not fully kept the Lord's covenant at all times, nor in all aspects of his life. It is clear that David was very concerned that Solomon would take his position in life seriously. Notice the "life-position" that David calls Solomon to be accountable for:

> As David's time to die drew near, he charged Solomon his son, saying, "I am going the way of all the earth. Be strong, therefore, and prove yourself a man. Keep the charge of the Lord your God. (1 Kings 2:1-3)

David did not tell Solomon to prove himself a king, nor did he tell him to prove himself a husband, or a father. He charged Solomon to prove himself to be a *man!* Furthermore, David goes on to tell Solomon to "keep the charge of the Lord."

Boys, hear the hearts of your fathers. We cry out with David, *"Keep the charge of the Lord."* Where do you start? How do you keep the charge? What is the charge? There are so many questions and so much to share with you that it would take much more than a book to communicate the wisdom of growing into manhood. It would take a lifetime, a lifetime that neither of us might have. Let us boil all of this down into a simple word or phrase that we can get our minds around so that we can understand how we are going to keep the charge. Let us simplify this into a simple word of wisdom that we can get our thoughts around so that we can understand what we are going to do to keep the charge. It is a word that we have already began to discuss—choices.

We are not talking about choosing where you will go, what you will eat, or what you will wear. We are not even talking about choosing between doing this or doing that, doing right or doing wrong. The choice we are talking about is much more fundamental than all of those. It is the choice that will determine the rest of your actions for all the days of your life. It is the choice that Joshua, the son of Nun, Moses' servant, put before the Israelites at Shechem:

> Now fear the Lord and serve him with all faithfulness. Throw away the gods your forefathers worshiped beyond the River and in Egypt, and serve the Lord. But if serving the Lord seems undesirable to you, then choose for yourselves this day whom you will serve, whether the gods your forefathers served beyond the River, or the gods of the Amorites, in whose land you are living. But as for me and my household, we will serve the Lord. (Joshua 24:14-15)

Whom will you serve? Your choices ought to glorify God and advance His kingdom. A decision is demanded. Too many people live their lives thinking that they do not have to make a decision about anything, most certainly not about God. This is dangerous thinking, because no decision is a decision. It is a decision not to serve God. Boys, the very first thing you must do in your journey to manhood is to decide whom you will serve, "the gods your forefathers served beyond the river, or the gods of the Amorites, in whose land you are living" or will you serve the Almighty God, the Creator of the heavens above and the earth below, the Father of our Lord and Savior Christ Jesus? This is a decision that you must make for yourself.

Boys, the charge we are placing before you demands your attention. It calls for you to transition from one phase of life to another, from being boys to being men. Yes, you are young—very young. Yes, we realize that you are not yet "men," but we know that it is never too early to start "chasing after God." It is time for you to renew your commitment to God. It is important to understand that every new phase of your spiritual journey will call for a new dimension of commitment. The choices you make as a believer are not about programs, processes, or styles. Boys, you are making decisions about your relationship with God—He is the *whom* of Joshua 24:15. Choose to serve God.

CALLED TO FEAR

Choosing to serve God, to follow Him, is not to be taken lightly. God is to be greatly feared, respected, and honored. He is worthy of all of that and much, much more. The author of Proverbs tells us, "The fear of the Lord is the beginning of knowledge" (Proverbs 1:7). God is to be feared. Such fear is healthy. After all, how can your finite brain ever comprehend an infinite God? He is indescribable. He is uncontainable. He is holy and separated from anything that we could ever hope to understand. God is not your buddy. He is not the old man upstairs, or the big guy up there. He is God. By definition, that means there is no other being like Him. He is all-powerful, all-knowing, and ever-present. He has no beginning, nor does He have an end. He is eternal.

Do you not love the way the prophet Isaiah describes his reaction to being in the presence of God? We want you to notice a few things from Isaiah 6:1-5:

- Isaiah saw the Lord seated high and exalted on a throne.
- Seraphs or Seraphim (heavenly beings who serve in the presence of the Lord) did not find being in the presence of God common or mundane. In fact, Isaiah states that they are in adoration to God's holiness (as witnessed by the covering of their face and feet, as well as their continual cries of "Holy! Holy! Holy!")
- Isaiah's initial response to seeing this heavenly scene was to fear, and fear greatly. Why? Isaiah realized the severity and the reality of his situation. Simply stated, God is holy and man is not. "Woe to me! I am ruined! For I am a man of unclean lips, and I live among a people of unclean lips, and my eyes have seen the King, the Lord Almighty" (Isaiah 6:5).

You are to fear the Lord your God, and this fear is to reveal itself in love. You are to love Him with all your heart, mind, and soul (Deuteronomy 6:4); and this love is to manifest itself by keeping His commandments (Exodus 20:6). It is important that you understand that what you fear will have power over you. Fear does not need to be grounded in truth or reality for it to have power over you. As long as you believe it to be true, that thing that you fear will have power over you. Allow us to illustrate this important fact with a story from Andy's childhood.

Duncan, you probably would not know it, but your grand-father (Papa Gowins) is a practical joker like you would not believe. When he used to take me wood duck hunting, he would tell me stories about a swamp creature that lived in the sloughs we hunted. It was part man, part Bigfoot, and a whole lot of bad. He would tell me these stories each morning as we were driving from the house to the sloughs (keep in mind this was before sunrise). The day I am thinking of was like any other day of duck hunting. Dad had shared the latest swamp-creature news with me on our morning commute to the sloughs; we had marched out into the murky, muddy waters of the fresh-water bog and had hunted for about an hour and a half; and I had kept my eyes open for both wood ducks and strange, unfamiliar movements in the water that might signal the coming of the swamp-creature. It was on our way back to the truck, while we were marching back through the sloughs, that *it* happened.

I had finally gotten out of the water and was walking on a bank of dry land that was about three feet wide. On both sides of this bank was water—deep, dark, muddy water. What happened next happened so fast that I am not even certain how to describe the sequence of events. Suddenly, there was a large splash to my right. As I started to turn to see the source of the noise, my dad

33

cried out, "Run! It's the swamp-thing!" With my heart in my throat and legs that felt like rubber, I started to move forward in slow motion. BAM! BAM! BAM! Dad unloaded his shotgun into the slough.

Now, by this time, everything had reverted back to real time. Dropping my shotgun (which was unloaded in its case), I ran forward straight into empty air, right off the left side of the embankment. The water on that side was at least four to five feet deep; I know that I ran off the bank, and I must have ran into the water. Now I do not claim to be divine, but I know of at least three people in history that have walked on water: Jesus, the Son of God; Simon Peter, Jesus' loudmouth disciple; and me, Andy Gowins, duck hunter and committed believer in the swamp-creature. I know you will not believe me, son, but I am telling you the truth. Even though I know I must have fallen into the water when I ran off the side of the bank, there was not a wet stitch of clothing on me. I ran across that slough straight for the truck.

I remember getting back to the truck believing that the swamp-creature had gotten my dad, only to hear him laughing and howling at the edge of the slough as he rolled around hysterically. It is true. What you fear controls you. If you fear monsters in your closet or under your bed, Bigfoot (or Little-feet), swamp-creatures, or space aliens, you will be a slave to that fear. If you fear sickness, death, relationships, love, commitment, or truth-telling, you will be captured by that fear and live every moment of life being ruled by it. Fear is defined as an unpleasant, often strong, emotion caused by anticipation (known or unknown anticipation). The Bible defines faith as "being sure of what we hope for and certain of what we do not see" (Hebrews 11:1). Faith and fear are two sides of the same coin. Have faith in God. Fear Him. Make a decision, this day, to follow Him. A decision to follow God is a decision to serve God.

God calls us to serve Him with deep sincerity, humility, and faithfulness. A decision to serve God is not just a decision to serve God; like any decision you will make, deciding to follow God and to serve Him has consequences. Those consequences will be evident in how you live out your decision to follow Him in every aspect and area of your life. Remember when we told you that this single decision was the fundamental, foundational decision that would guide your life? When you determine to serve God it will require that you set your house in order; it will require some housecleaning.

God is a jealous God. He will not tolerate any other gods, regardless of how big or how small a god it may be. "You shall have no other gods before me. You shall not make for yourself an idol in the form of anything...you shall not bow down to them or worship them; for I, the Lord your God, am a jealous God" (Exodus 20:3-5). Of course the age-old question is, "What is an idol?" An idol is anything that distracts you from devoting yourself wholly and fully to the person and the service of the Lord your God. Just as God is jealous for your attention, we want you to be jealous for His attention. We want you to be jealous for His honor and His reputation.

Fear the Lord, choose to serve Him, and throw away your idols. We desire for you to make a declaration that is final and resolved that echoes the words of Joshua, "As for me and my

35

house, we will serve the Lord." Boys, true service for God comes out of a true heart of worship. True worship comes out of an honest understanding of who God is and who He has called you to be.

CALLED TO BE HOLY

We have all heard the charge against "those holier than thou Christians." When we call you to live a holy life, we are not calling you to be a hypocrite, one of those "holier than thou" people. We are calling you to a life that seeks to be transformed into the very image of Christ in every manner possible (Romans 12:2). Holiness is not a mystical marker of your Christian identity; it does not enable you to walk five feet off the ground or wear a halo. Holiness is all about character. It comes with having the right priorities and making the right decisions. Remember, it is all about the choices. Furthermore, God expects you to be holy just as He is holy. He has set you apart so that you can be like Him.

You might say, "But Dad, no one can be like God. Can they?" Look at what the apostle Paul states in Colossians 3:1-17.

Since, then, you have been raised with Christ, set your hearts on things above, where Christ is seated at the right hand of God. Set your minds on things above, not on earthly things. For you died and your life is now hidden with Christ in God. When Christ, who is your life, appears, then you also will appear with him in glory. Put to death, therefore, whatever belongs to your earthly nature:

sexual immorality, impurity, lust, evil desires and greed which is idolatry. Because of these, the wrath of God is coming. You used to walk in these ways, in the life you once lived. But now you must rid yourselves of all such things as these: anger, rage, malice, slander, and filthy language from your lips. Do not lie to each other, since you have taken off your old self with its practices and have put on the new self, which is being renewed in knowledge in the image of its Creator. Here there is no Greek or Jew, circumcised or uncircumcised, barbarian, Scythian, slave or free, but Christ is all, and is in all. Therefore, as God's chosen people, holy and dearly loved, clothe yourselves with compassion, kindness, humility, gentleness and patience. Bear with each other and forgive whatever grievances you may have against one another. Forgive as the Lord forgave you. And over all these virtues put on love, which binds them all together in perfect unity. Let the peace of Christ rule in your hearts, since as members of one body you were called to peace. And be thankful. Let the word of Christ dwell in you richly as you teach and admonish one another with all wisdom, and as you sing psalms, hymns and spiritual songs with gratitude in your hearts to God. And whatever you do, whether in word or deed, do it all in the name of the Lord Jesus, giving thanks to God the Father through him.

According to this passage, if you have truly been "born again" and have been "raised up with Christ," you are to "set your mind on the things above, not on the things of the earth." Why? You can set your mind on the things above because you have put to death your old self, your old nature. You are a new creature in Christ Jesus (2 Corinthians 5:17). Notice what Verse 5 says you can put to death: immorality, impurity, passion, evil desire, and greed; also anger, wrath, malice, slander, abusive speech, and lying. But the apostle Paul just does not tell you what you are delivered from; he goes on to tell you what you are delivered into: compassion, kindness, humility, gentleness, patience, love, peace, thankfulness, and wisdom (Colossians 3:10-16). You are part of a chosen race, a royal priesthood, a holy nation, a people for God's own possession (1 Peter 2:9). 1 Peter 1:13-16 states that you have been set apart.

Therefore, prepare your minds for action, keep sober in spirit, fix your hope completely on the grace to be brought to you at the revelation of Christ Jesus. As obedient children, do not be conformed to the former lusts which were yours in your ignorance, but like the Holy One who called you, be holy yourselves also in all your behavior; because it is written, "You shall be holy, for I am holy."

Being holy, having the very character and mind of Christ, is a difficult task. In fact, if you are not very careful to closely examine your life as a Christian, then it is possible to fool even yourself into believing that you are doing all right. Keeping the charge to be holy, so that you can prove yourself a man, requires that you take a deep introspective investigation of your Christian life on a regular basis. While we do not believe that good works or good deeds can save you (salvation is from God and God alone, through grace and grace alone), we do believe that Pastor James is correct, "faith without works is dead" (James 2:26). There must be visible and tangible evidence of your salvation, and this evidence must be manifested through your good works and good deeds. Where did James get such an idea? He must have been listening to his big brother (well, his big half-brother). Jesus stated the same message in the parable found in John 15:1-11. Jesus is the vine. His followers are the branches, and the branches are distinguished by the fruit they bear.

CALLED TO BEAR FRUIT

Boys, as Christians it is easy to engage in a flurry of activities that appear to promote your spiritual growth. We go to church regularly, become active in ministry, attend seminars, give of our money and our time, and when it is all said and done, we wonder why our relationship with Jesus seems so shallow and superficial. It is easy to have a superficial relationship with Christ, giving the appearance of being connected to Him. Our hope and desire for you on your journey to true manhood is that you would never have to experience such a hypocritical paradox. Listen to the wisdom of your fathers. Do not overlook the obvious; do not neglect the One who is the source of your life—Christ Jesus, your Lord and Savior. In the fifteenth chapter of the gospel of John, Jesus lays down a basic biblical principle for how you can know him better and in the process become a fruitful disciple.

Abide in Me, and I in you. As the branch cannot bear
fruit of itself unless it abides in the vine, so neither can
you unless you abide in Me. I am the vine and you are
the branches; he who abides in Me and I in him; he bears
much fruit, for apart from Me you can do nothing. (John
15:4-5)

This is the seventh and the last of the "I am" statements
(statements Jesus made concerning His divine identity: John
6:35, I am the bread of life; 9:5, I am the light of the world; 10:7,
I am the gate; 10:11, I am the good shepherd; 11:25, I am the resurrection; 14:6, I am the way and the truth and the life; and 15:1,
I am the vine). In this agricultural metaphor, Jesus describes four
basic characters:

- The vine (Jesus Christ) - Jesus is the *true vine*; He is the
  one perfect, essential, and enduring vine before which all
  other vines were and are but dim shadows.
- The branches (believers)—The followers of Christ (you
  and me) are described as the branches.
- The vinedresser (God)—The Father is referred to as the
  Gardener. What does the Father do in His role as the
  Gardner/Vinedresser? Most translations state that He
  cuts off those branches that do not bear fruit; however,
  the Greek word *airo*, which lies behind the verb being
  translated "to cut off," may also mean "to lift up or to
  pick up." Actually, this translation makes more sense,
  since this would be the natural or normal sequence of

events for taking care of the vines. Grapes must hang free from the branches if they are to grow properly; any branch that trails on the ground becomes unproductive. It is the role of the vinedresser to lift up the branches, to secure them and support them, so as to encourage their growth. This is what the Gardner does, He lifts up the branches (you and me) so that they can develop and mature properly. However, that is not the Father's only role. He also purges or prunes the branches. The Greek word used here, *katharizo,* means to cleanse, make clean, or purify. This act of purging is accomplished by God as He removes that which is spiritually detrimental in a believer's life. The Father washes or cleanses the branches so that they can be more productive and bear more fruit. As He trims and prunes those branches that are not producing fruit, He is getting rid of the dead wood in the believer's life. The process of pruning may be painful, but it is for the believer's own good (Hebrews 12:10). The manner in which this cleansing is accomplished is by the Word of God (Psalm 119:9; John 15:3).

- The fruit (the proof)—What is the fruit? The fruit is nothing less than the outcome of persevering dependence on the vine, driven by faith, embracing all of the believer's life and the product of his witness. Several different kinds of spiritual fruit are named in the New Testament:
  ◊ Winning others to Christ (Romans 1:13)
  ◊ Growing in holiness and obedience (Romans 6:22)

41

◊ Christian giving (Romans 15:28)

◊ The fruit of the Spirit (Galatians 5:22-23)

◊ Good works and service (Colossians 1:10)

◊ Praise that comes from our hearts and lips
   (Hebrews 13:15)

◊ Peace (John 14:27)

◊ Love and joy (John 15:9-11)

Boys, essential to understanding this passage is the fact that as the branches we are to abide or remain in the true vine, who is Christ. The word *abide* (or remain) is used eleven times in John 15:1-11. It is the key word in this passage, detailing what it requires to produce good fruit. You must remain in the vine/ Jesus. The secret of fruitfulness is the activity of abiding in Christ. You are to live your life in such a manner that it invites Christ Jesus to abide with you. Jesus is very quick to state that no branch can bear fruit in isolation. It must have a vital connection to the vine. No branch has life in itself; it is utterly dependent for life and fruitfulness on the vine to which it is connected. Apart from Christ you are able to do nothing.

You must be rightly related to Jesus. The imagery of the vine and the branches suggests incorporation and mutual indwelling. The branches derive their life from the vine; the vine produces its fruit through the branches. Fruitfulness is the unmistakable and infallible mark of true Christianity. To be a fruitless Christian is to be a contradiction. The apparent purpose of these verses is to insist that there are no true Christians without some measure of fruit. Abiding or remaining in Him means to keep in fellowship with Christ so that His life can work in and through you to produce fruit. Remaining in Him certainly involves the Word of God and the confession of sin so that nothing hinders our communion with Him. It also involves obeying Him simply because we love Him. This relationship must be cultivated in your life. It is not automatic. If you are to abide in Christ, you must worship Him, meditate upon God's Word, pray, practice sacrificial giving (stewardship), and serve Him.

Of course the important question is, "How can I tell if I am abiding in Christ?" The Bible is very clear on this issue; there are special evidences that appear, and they are unmistakably clear. When you are abiding in Christ, you will produce fruit (John 15:2). When you are producing fruit, you will also experience the Father's pruning, in order that you might bear more fruit (John 15:2). According to John 15:7, when you are abiding in Christ, you will have your prayers answered and you will experience a deepening love for Christ and for others believers as well. You will also experiences joy (John 15:11).

We do not want to dwell too long on this metaphor, but notice what Jesus says in Matthew 7:17-20, "So every good tree bears good fruit, but the bad tree bears bad fruit...Every tree that does not bear good fruit is cut down and thrown into the fire. So then, you will know them by their fruits." You are called to bear fruit and to bear much fruit. This is how Jesus glorifies the Father. By being a fruitful believer, you help Jesus glorify His heavenly Father. When the vine bears much fruit, God is glorified.

The fruit that Jesus speaks of is the by-product of His control in your life. If the fruit is to grow in your life, then you must

43

join your life with Christ's (John 15:4-5). You must know Him, love Him, and imitate Him. As a Christian, your actions should reflect your faith. Your relationship with Jesus can be described in terms of your obedience, perseverance, love, fruitfulness, dependence, union, and even pruning/maturing.

It is this process of pruning or growing that will help you to abide in Him. Boys, wisdom is gained through a constant process of growing. Wisdom begins with trusting and honoring God. Next, you must realize that the Bible is God's wisdom revealed to you for the purpose of righteous instruction. Third, and we cannot stress this enough, it is all about the choices you make in life; you must make a life-long series of right choices, avoiding moral pitfalls. Finally, when you mess things up and make a sinful or mistaken choice, learn from your error, correct it, and move on (Proverbs 2:9-10). Keep the charge. You be holy!

Life Application Questions:
Chapter 2

1) Have you ever faced a faith-testing decision like Joshua asked of the Hebrews in Joshua 24:14-15? Did you pass or fail this test? What lesson did you learn?

2) Why do so many people live with no fear of God? What implications does this fact have for future generations?

3) We list fruit that should be evident in the life of a Christian. Review this list on page 28 and honestly reveal the areas in which you are the strongest and weakest.

44

HELPFUL HINT

Do something "fruity" with your son.

- Visit a nursing home resident.
- Contact your pastor to inquire about areas in which the two of you can serve the church together, e.g. cleaning, welcoming visitors. Afterwards discuss the fruit that was displayed in that act or service.

Duncan and Dakota (Andy's children) on vacation at Disney World

CHAPTER THREE

Walk in His Ways—Being a Disciplined Man of Character

On his deathbed, David commanded his son to prove that he was a man by doing all that the Lord required. This begs the question, "What does the Lord require?" The Lord required that Solomon "walk in his ways," keeping the commandments. But, what does it mean, to "walk in his ways"? This phrase is evidently tied to the action of keeping God's decrees, commands, laws, and requirements, but is this the totality of "walking in his ways"?

The Pharisees were well known for how they kept every nuance of the Law, yet Jesus would say to them, "Woe to you, teachers of the law and Pharisees, you hypocrites!" (Matthew 23:25). Their actions made them appear righteous, but their hearts were darkened with sin. "You are like whitewashed tombs, which look beautiful on the outside, but on the inside are full of dead men's bones and everything unclean. In the same way, on the outside you appear to people as righteous, but on the inside you are full of hypocrisy and wickedness" (Matthew 23:27-28). In fact, Jesus would illustrate how dangerous it is to act the part, "You snakes! You brood of vipers! How will you escape being condemned to hell?" (Matthew 23:33). Yes, "walking in his ways" does involve obedience to God's commandments, but it also demands a conversion and a transformation of the very essence, the very core of each and every man. Walking in his ways demands a heart that is bent toward God.

When David charged Solomon to "walk in his ways," he was instructing him to be a man of righteous character. It is the heart that dictates character. "The things that come out of the mouth come from the heart, and these make a man 'unclean.' For out of the heart come evil thoughts, murder, adultery, sexual immorality, theft, false testimony, slander" (Matthew 15:18-19). Character is determined by the passions of your heart. This is why the psalmist would write, "Blessed is the man [whose]...delight is in the law of the Lord...on His law he meditates day and night" (Psalm 1:1-2). People are motivated by what they think is important, whether or not that perception is true; "For as he thinks within himself, so he is" (Proverbs 23:7). How do you "walk in his ways?" You must "love the Lord your God, with all your heart and with all your soul and with all your mind" (Matthew 22:37). It is the echo of Deuteronomy 10:12-13:

> And now, O Israel, what does the Lord your God ask of you but to fear the Lord your God, to walk in all his ways, to love him, to serve the Lord your God with all your heart and with all your soul, and to observe the Lord's commands and decrees that I am giving you today for your own good.

And again in Deuteronomy 30:15-16:

> See, I set before you today life and prosperity, death and

destruction. For I command you today to love the Lord your God, to walk in his ways, and to keep his commands, decrees and laws; then you will live and increase, and the Lord your God will bless you in the land you are entering to possess.

"Walking in his ways" produces happiness.

- "Blessed are all who fear the Lord, who walk in his ways" (Psalm 128:1).
- "Blessed are they whose ways are blameless, who walk according to the law of the Lord. Blessed are they who keep his statutes and seek him with all their heart. They do nothing wrong; they walk in his ways" (Psalm 119:1-3).

"Walking in his ways" demands Godly character.

GODLY CHARACTER

Boys, these thoughts are not easy to put down on paper but we have to, because you must know how important it is to us that you grow up to be men of great character and integrity—real men. Even as we put these thoughts to paper, we can hear your questions: "But Dad, how do we prove ourselves to be men? What is the mark of true manhood? How do we bear good fruit, righteous fruit that shows that we're 'abiding in Christ'? What does abiding mean? What is Godly character?"

Character is not easily defined. You just know it when you see it. The term *character* can mean many things. *Webster's* defines character as a conventionalized graphic device placed on an object as an indication of ownership, origin, or relationship. "WHAT? Dad, I'm just a kid. What does all that mean, and who is Webster?" Character is like the sign that sits on the front lawn of the church. It identifies exactly who you are. It shows from where you came and to whom you belong. As young, maturing believers, you must remember that you are called to live in the world, but to not be of the world; "Do not love the world nor the things in the world" (1 John 2:15). To whom does your sign say that you belong?

"But Dad, what is character?" Not only is character defined as an identification marker, it is also defined as one of the attributes or features that make up and distinguish an individual. It is a feature that separates or distinguishes you from others; it is a description of your main or essential nature. According to God's Word, all have sinned (Romans 3:23) and all are under the curse and consequence of that sin (1 Corinthians 15:21-22). Your "essential nature" before Christ was that of sin (1 Corinthians 6:9-10; Galatians 5:19-21); but because of the grace of God (Romans 5:8) and of Christ's Holy Spirit dwelling inside you, now you have the hope of 1 Corinthians 6:11, "Such were some of you; but you were washed, but you were sanctified, but you were justified in the name of the Lord Jesus Christ and in the Spirit of our God." Even now, as maturing believers, each of you possesses the very mind of Christ (1 Corinthians 2:16). The reality of God's truth teaches us that there are really only two essential natures—that which serves the lusts or deeds of the flesh, and that which is characterized by those who walk in the Spirit.

50

Character can also refer to one's position, one's reputation, and even one's identification and practice of moral excellence and moral firmness. Henry and Tom Blackaby define character like this:

> The development of a strong Christian character is the development of a man after God's own heart. Your character is who you are when no one is looking and what you are willing to stand for when someone is looking. Character is who you are striving to be and what you can be trusted with. (Blackaby, 1998, p. 9)

Character is how you live your life when others are watching, as well as when they are not watching. Men of Godly character possess a heart that is responsive to God and lives that are obedient to God. Men of Godly character have lives that are characterized by integrity that honors God. To have integrity implies wholeness. It is saying that you are a whole person. Integrity is making choices—not just good choices, but choices that do not cause "cracks" or "chips" that split apart your wholeness as a person. When you deliberately do what you know is wrong, you spoil your integrity, your wholeness. "Integrity of character occurs when there is consistency between actions and inner convictions over time" (Blackaby, p. 9).

All you have is your personal integrity and your character; guard them carefully. Protect your good name and your reputation at all costs. Remember, however, your good name involves and includes more than just your family name. You have also identified yourself as a follower of Christ—one of His beloved children. Be diligent to protect the good name of Christ Jesus in all that you do. Boys, protect your witness at all cost. Be men of great character; be men of Godly character.

On his deathbed, King David charged Solomon, his son, to be strong and to "prove" that he (Solomon) was a man by keeping "the charge of the Lord your God, to walk in His ways" (1 Kings 2:3). It is the charge to exhibit Godly character. It is the charge we give to you. Be strong and prove that you are a man by being a man of Christ-like character. Godly, biblical character is exhibiting the very character of Christ (Galatians 5:22).

LIFE IN THE SPIRIT

In his letter to the Galatians, Paul encouraged the church at Galatia to walk in the Spirit. Biblically, the concept of "walking" when used in such a manner (i.e., walking in the Spirit, walking in his ways) is implicit of the concept of living one's life according to the stated directive. Paul wants the Galatians to live according to the freedom they have been given in Christ.

Because of Jesus' saving work on the cross, those who have believed in their hearts and confessed with their mouths that Jesus is Lord (Romans 10:9), have been released from the consequences of the law and have been given the ability to love. However, even though we want to please God, even though we want to love God by obeying Him, our sin nature continually pulls us into disobedience. This is the reality of the human condition. "I do not understand what I do. For what I want to do I do not do, but what I hate I do" (Romans 7:15). How then do you experience a life released from the restrictions of God's law? How do you guard against becoming a "whitewashed tomb," like the hypocritical Pharisees of Jesus' day?

The answer to this battle between your old and new nature is found in the inward ministry of the Holy Spirit. To experience victory over the desires of the flesh (Galatians 5:19-21), you must live or walk by the Spirit. Jesus has called us to live each day under the control of the Holy Spirit. Life under the control of the Spirit is what God intends for the Christian. Paul directs his readers to walk by the Spirit instead of indulging the desires of the flesh. If you follow Paul's teaching, the Spirit will create in you a set of qualities that are collectively referred to as the "fruit of the Spirit" (Galatians 5:22-23).

This means having the Word of Christ in your mind. God's Word is an agent of transformation, "Do not conform any longer to the pattern of this world, but be transformed by the renewing of your mind" (Romans 12:2). It is a guard against disobedience, "I have hidden your word in my heart that I might not sin against you" (Psalm 119:11). Through the Holy Spirit, Christ enables our minds to understand the truth of Scripture. According to 1 Corinthians 3:10-16, the natural man, sinful man, cannot understand the things that come from the Spirit of God, but the regenerate, born-again, man, through the ministry of the Spirit, is able to understand what God has freely given to him.

Living under the control of Christ's Spirit also means having the love of Christ in your heart. It is the love of Christ that guides one's actions. The Spirit works in our hearts to cause us to want to do the things God wants us to do. "It is God who works in you to will...his good purpose" (Philippians 2:13). Living under the control of the Spirit enables you to have the power of Christ in your character. The Spirit empowers us to be transformed into the very character of God/Jesus, to live the life Christ would live if He were in our shoes. By the ministry of the indwelling Holy Spirit, "we...are being transformed into his likeness with ever-increasing glory, which comes from the Lord, who is the Spirit" (2 Corinthians 3:18). "Strong Christian character is both the result of human effort and divine intervention (1 Corinthians 15:10). It is the work of God as you relate to Him in love. Strong Christian character is the result of your heart's desire to obey God (Philippians 2:12-13)." (Blackaby, p. 9) The Bible commands us to put on Christ (Galatians 3:27), to clothe ourselves with Christ (Romans 13:14), and to conform to the likeness of Christ (Romans 8:29). These commands are God's strategy, His method to help us experience the full and abundant life Christ has to offer.

Boys, you have been created in the image of God (Genesis 1:27). It is not a physical image. God does not have a physical form, but rather you have been created according to the image of His purpose. The essence of manhood, or masculinity, is not found in how a man looks, but rather who a man is. Who a man is, is revealed in what a man does—his actions, and this according to his character. Thus, we return full circle to the reality that it is the desires of your heart, your passions that will establish the "plumb line" of your character.

The qualities of Godly character include a heart set upon holiness. A heart that is humble, repentant, and pure. Such a heart fears the Lord because it understands not only who God is, but also what God demands. Because He is holy, God will not tolerate sin. A heart set upon holiness fears sin and its consequences. A heart devoted to God is steadfast, dedicated, dependable, and worthy of trust. It is an obedient heart that is submissive to the instruction of His authority. The man with a holy heart chases after God. All of these qualities should create a man of character who is seeking and loving God. "If…you seek the Lord your God, you will find him if you look for him with all your heart and with all your soul" (Deuteronomy 4:29). The Lord your God is a jealous God, and He demands your complete loyalty and love. His holiness demands your holiness. It demands that you walk in His ways, that you live by His Spirit. Living by the Spirit enables us to fulfill the law of love; it enables us to overcome the desires of the flesh; and it allows us to produce fruit. The "fruit of the Spirit" cannot in its entirety be produced in human lives without the help of the Holy Spirit. They, the nine qualities of "the fruit of the Spirit," are a supernatural work. (Erickson, 1992, p. 280)

The New Testament speaks of several different kinds of fruit: people won to Christ, holy living, gifts brought to God, good works, and praise. These are some of the "fruit" that Jesus is talking about in John 15:5, "I am the vine; you are the branches. If a man remains in me and I in him, he will bear much fruit; apart from me you can do nothing." We want you to "abide in Christ" by living according to God's commandments and to "bear" all of these fruits in your life. In order to produce these fruits, however, you must first bear the fruit of the Spirit (Galatians 5:22-23), which is the manifestation of Godly, Christ-like character. The apostle Paul states in Galatians 2:20, "I have been crucified with Christ and I no longer live, but Christ lives in me. The life I live in the body, I live by faith in the Son of God, who loved me and gave himself for me." When you became a Christian, you died to yourself. You died so that Christ could live through you. You were raised to a new life, and because of this amazing fact, you no longer live for yourself but for Christ. When you were "saved" you took into your life all that God is (Father, Son, and Spirit), and now the Spirit is helping to build Godly character in you. "You build character as you would an altar or building; block upon block, decision upon decision, line upon line, little upon little." (Cole, 1992, p. 81) When you walk in the ways of God, according to Galatians 5:22-23, the Holy Spirit will produce the qualities of Godliness in your life. The characteristics that God wants in your life are seen in the nine-fold fruit of the Spirit: love, joy, peace, patience, kindness, goodness, faithfulness, gentleness, and self-control. The apostle Paul states that the fruit of the Spirit commences with love; all of the other fruit is really an outgrowth of love.

Compare these eight qualities with the characteristics of love given to the Corinthians (1 Corinthians 13:4-8). God's divine love is patient, kind; it is not envious, not boastful, not proud, not rude, not self-seeking, not easily angered; it keeps no record of wrongs; it does not delight in evil; it rejoices in the truth; it protects, trusts, hopes, and perseveres; it never fails. This divine love is God's gift to us, and we must cultivate it and pray that it will increase. When a person lives in the sphere of love, then he can experience the rest of the fruit of the Spirit.

Boys, do you live your life in the sphere of love? Can it be said of you that you are patient and kind? Are you easily angered; do you keep a record of all those who have done you wrong? Do you find your joy in doing what is right or do you delight in doing that which is evil, wicked, or perverse? Are you men who protect, who are trustworthy, who hope, and persevere to the end? Does the fruit of the Spirit illustrate your character?

THE FRUIT OF THE SPIRIT (GALATIANS 5:22-23)

Boys, show the world that you are men—men of Godly character, men whose character mirrors the very character of God. There are many ways to describe the characteristics of God. His characteristics are also called His attributes. "When we speak of the attributes of God, we are referring to those qualities of God which constitute what He is; they are the very characteristics of his nature." (Erickson, 89) What is God's nature?

- The Creator God is independent (Acts 17:24-25; Job 41:11; Psalm 50:10-12).
- He is unchangeable (Psalm 102:25-27; Malachi 3:6; James 1:17).
- He is eternal (Psalm 90:2; Revelations 1:8; Psalm 90:4; Galatians 4:4-5; Acts 17:30-31).
- He is almighty or omnipotent (all-powerful) (Jeremiah 23:24).
- He is omnipresent (Genesis 1:1; Deuteronomy 10:14; Jeremiah 23:23-24; Psalm 139:7-10; 1 Kings 8:27; Amos 9:1-4).

57

- He is unified, even as He is triune (Father, Son, and Holy Spirit). (Deuteronomy 6:4-5; Isaiah 44:6-45; 25; Mark 12:29-30; 1 Corinthians 8:4; Ephesians 4:6; 1 Timothy 2:5).
- He is transcendent (Isaiah 66:1).
- He is spiritual by nature.
- He is sovereign (Daniel 4:34).
- He reigns.
- He is omniscient (all-knowing); He sees and knows all things (Proverbs 15:3).
- He is holy (Leviticus 11:44).
- He is good.
- He is love (Psalm 136:1).

God's characteristics, however, are not descriptive of His character. God's character is best illustrated in the life of Christ. Jesus Christ was and is the Anointed One of Israel—the Messiah. He is co-equal and co-eternal with God the Father. He is the preexistent, divine son of God (John 1:1; 8:58), born of the Virgin (Isaiah 7:14; Matthew 1:16), who took upon himself the nature of humanity. Being co-equal with the Father, he possesses all the attributes of God. He is "perfect in Godhead and also perfect in manhood; truly God and truly man" (Anthony, 2001, p. 37). Jesus was a man's man—honest, gentle, compassionate, loving, firm, and devoted to God the Father. You would do well to mimic Christ. In fact, the descriptive name of Christian means to be Christ-like in how you live your life in both your character and in your actions.

In his letter to the Galatians, Paul lists nine qualities that the Spirit-filled and the Spirit-controlled believer should have in his life. He calls them the fruit of the Spirit. These nine qualities describe the very character of God (Galatians 5:22-23): love, joy, peace, patience, kindness, goodness, faithfulness, gentleness, and self-control. The fruit of the Spirit refers to the tangible example of the Spirit's work in the believer's life—in your lives! Is there evidence of the Spirit's work in your lives? The fruit of the Spirit is the by-product of one's submission to Christ's control. According to John 15:4-5, you must join your life with Christ's; you must abide (live) in Christ if the fruit is to grow in your life. It is not about having each and every fruit perfectly modeled in your life; it is about having these attitudes and behaviors that generally characterize your life. You must know Him, love Him, and imitate Him. If the Holy Spirit is genuinely at work in your life, He will be producing the kind of character traits that Paul calls "the fruit of the Spirit."

These nine Spirit-given characteristics are the real evidence of the Spirit's work in a Christian's life. Love, joy, and peace in your life are the most certain signs of a vital and vibrant relationship with the Lord your God. The apostle Paul, however, stresses the primacy of love over all other spiritual gifts and/or fruit, "But the greatest of these is love" (1 Corinthians 13:13). "In fact, judging by his highlighting of love in Galatians 5, as well as later in 1 Corinthians 13, Paul saw all the other virtues listed in the fruit of the Spirit as included in and springing from this first-listed virtue"—love *(agape)* (Longnecker, 1990, p. 260).

THE FRUIT OF LOVE

What we describe as love is differentiated in Greek by three various expressions: *phileo, eros,* and *agapao. Phileo* is the most commonly used word for love in the Greek New Testament, indicating a general attraction toward a person or thing. It is commonly interpreted as familial love, intimate friendship, and even fondness. *Eros,* on the other hand, indicates a love which desires to passionately possess. In Galatians 5:22, Paul uses the word *agapao.* In the New Testament, *agapao* and the noun *agape* have taken on a particular significance in that they are used to speak of the sacrificial love of God as well as the Christian way of life based on God's love.

The incomprehensible love of God is to be the controlling force of the Christian life; and because of that love, the Spirit-filled believer is to be the living, breathing example of God's love to both the church and to the non-believing world. Love is the mortar that holds the Christian life together. Are you the living, breathing example of God's divine love? "For God so loved the world that he gave his one and only Son, that whoever..." (John 3:16). Are you a whoever "lover"? It is easy to pick and choose whom you will love; it is Godly to love everyone that the Lord your God places in your path. You asked earlier, "How do I prove myself to be a man?" Make Godly, self-sacrificing love for others the cornerstone of your character. Walk in the way of love!

Do you remember the true Bible story of the teacher that comes to ask Jesus what the greatest of all the commandments is? It is a trick. It is a trap. If Jesus names one commandment more important than another, then the authority of God is in question. Thinking carefully, Jesus answers the teacher,

> Love the Lord your God with all your heart and with all your soul and with all your mind. This is the first and greatest commandment. And the second is like it: Love your neighbor as yourself. All the Law and the Prophets hang on these two commandments. (Matthew 22:37-40)

Wow! Did you hear what Jesus said? The entire law, all of "His statutes, His commandments, His ordinances, and His testimonies," hinges upon love. Why? Because "God is love; whoever lives in love lives in God, and God in him" (1 John 4:17). It is impossible to be a man of Christ-like character without the foundation of love. "Dear friends, let us love one another, for love comes from God. Everyone who loves has been born of God and knows God. Whoever does not love does not know God, because God is love" (1 John 4:7-8). "Okay, that's easy enough, Dad. But what does love look like in the life of the Spirit-filled man? How will I 'prove myself a man' by showing love?" you ask.

Have you ever noticed that the Old Testament writers were very careful in using the word love in describing their relationship with God? In fact, when you look at the original language of the Old Testament it is very difficult, if not nearly impossible, to find a passage where the writer boldly states, or even suggests, that he, or the people of God, loves God. The closest you will come to finding such a passage, in the original language, is the use of love to communicate the concept of "like" or "intense, impassioned friendship." Why?

The answer is clearly given in the law. "Love the Lord your God and keep his requirements, his decrees, his laws and his commands always" (Deuteronomy 11:1). The conjunction "and" in this directive is not connecting two separate thoughts; it is bridging the commandment. How do you love the Lord your God? You keep His commandments. It is reiterated in Joshua 22:5, "But be very careful to keep the commandment and the law that Moses the servant of the Lord gave you: to love the Lord your God, to walk in all his ways, to obey his commands, to hold fast to him and to serve him with all your heart and all your soul." The Old Testament writers understood the concept of "loving" as "obeying." This is why they could not bring themselves to write that the people of God loved Him, because they were not obeying Him. What does all of this have to do with "walking in His ways"? It is not enough to say that you love God; you must obey Him. If there is any doubt or confusion left concerning this very important point, then look at what Jesus had to say about loving and obeying. "If you *love me,* you *will obey* what I command" (John 14:15, emphasis added). Take note boys, not "you might obey" or "you can choose what to obey"; nor did He say, "It would be a good idea to obey." Jesus said, "You will obey." His directive leaves very little room for discussion.

We see this Old Testament principle come to life right in front of our eyes in the New Testament. In John 21, we witness this scene on the shores of Lake Tiberias. Jesus is sitting with Peter asking him the most haunting of questions, "Peter, do you love me?" Twice Jesus asks Peter this question, using the Greek word *"agape"* for love. He uses the Greek word for the sacrificial love of God, which produces the love that is expressed by the Christian way of life, "If you *agape* me, you will keep my command." Each time Peter asserts, "Yes, Lord you know that I *philo* (love) you" (John 21:15). Peter cannot bring himself to say that he loves Jesus in a divine, self-sacrificing manner; after all, Peter had denied Jesus three times. At best, Peter loves Jesus as he would love his own flesh and blood. It is the best that Peter can do. Why? Peter could not say that he loved (*agape*) Jesus, because he had not been faithful nor obedient to "walk in His ways." If you are going to be a man of Christ-like character and integrity, you will be a man who understands this simple biblical principle of loving and obeying.

Be bold in your love. It is because of love that Paul can say to Timothy, "For God has not given us [you] a spirit of timidity, but of power and love and discipline. Therefore do not be ashamed of the testimony of our Lord or of me His prisoner, but join with me in suffering for the gospel according to the power of God" (2 Timothy 1:7-8). So, be bold in the Lord! As you grow into manhood, we want you to be men of boldness and yet, in your strength, men of character, compassion, mercy, and empathy. We do not want you to be afraid to announce your love and obedience to the Lord God. "Christian love is not flabby nor is it sentimental; it is keenly perceptive, capable of true discrimination (Philippians 1:9). Christian love does not refrain from the ministry of accountability, when such is demanded by the situation (2 Corinthians 2:4)" (Fung, 1988, p. 264).

What does love look like? The Christ-like believer demonstrates his love for others by having a servant's attitude, which manifests itself in service to others. Notice what the apostle Paul has to say about love just a few verses before he introduces the fruit of the Spirit:

> You, my brothers, were called to be free. But do not use your freedom to indulge the sinful nature; rather, serve one another in love. The entire law is summed up in a single command: "Love your neighbor as yourself." If you keep on biting and devouring each other, watch out or you will be destroyed by each other. (Galatians 5:13-15)

Serving others in love with an attitude of humility and submission ought to be the natural response of the Spirit-filled Christian as he expresses the freedom he has in Christ. Paul also paints a picture for us as to what love is not, "biting and devouring each other." The legalists, who had infiltrated the church at Galatia, were dividing the fellowship. Because of "biting and devouring of each other," the church and community of faith were on the verge of destruction. Such action is not a demonstration of what love *ought* to be producing in the lives of born-again believers. Christ gives you the freedom to love others truly. Paul states that Christian freedom is the right and the privilege of every believer. You are called to serve others. Your faith should be expressing itself through love; serving, not sinning; living free from the desires of the flesh.

WHAT DOES LOVE LOOK LIKE?

So what does love look like in the life of the believer who is abiding in Christ? Let us look at a few Bible verses to see how God's Word describes the loving believer. As we have already seen, we are called to love God and love our neighbors, but Jesus in His Sermon on the Mount gave a new definition to the concept of neighbor. "You have heard that it was said, Love your neighbor and hate your enemy. But I tell you: Love your enemies and pray for those who persecute you" (Matthew 5:43). It is easy to love those who love you, who are like you, and/or who you want to love. God's divine love, however, demands that you love the unlovable and the undesirable. "But God demonstrates his own love for us in this: While we were still sinners, Christ died for us" (Romans 5:8).

What does love look like? In 1 Peter 2:17, the apostle would write, "Show proper respect to everyone: Love the brotherhood of believers, fear God, honor the king." The Christ-like man who is "walking in His ways" demonstrates love by appreciating all people. After all, man has been created in the image of God. He loves the church and fears God. The Spirit-filled believer respects the authorities that God has placed over him. In other words, love does not know the boundaries of saved or unsaved. Love is not a respecter of position; love recognizes the validity and truth of Exodus 20:2-3, "I am the Lord your God, who brought you out of Egypt, out of the land of slavery. You shall have no other gods before me."

What does love look like in the life of a Spirit-filled man of integrity? Love is the secret of unity. It begins with love for fellow

Christians and extends to all people. He loves the brethren. His affinity is for the Church. Jesus stated, "A new command I give you: Love one another. As I have loved you, so you must love one another. By this all men will know that you are my disciples, if you love one another" (John 13:34-35); and again in John 15:17, "This is my command: Love each other." If there is any doubt, look at what the apostle Peter says: "Now that you have purified yourselves by obeying the truth so that you have sincere love for your brothers, love one another deeply, from the heart." Why are we to love deeply? We are to love deeply, "Because you have been born again, not of perishable seed, but of imperishable, through the living and enduring word of God" (1 Peter 1:22-23). You are to love the Church "deeply" because Christ loves His Bride. He loves her so much that He gave himself for her. Prove thyself a man and take to heart the warning of 1 Corinthians 16:13-14, "Be on your guard; stand firm in the faith; be men of courage; be strong. Do everything in love."

To love God is to obey God. To obey God is to deny one's self, not of outward things; but rather it is the denial of what one thinks, feels, or wants that is in opposition to the Word of God. Denial is not to push down one's emotions, but it is to deny one's selfish will. It is putting "self" to death. "The man who loves his life will lose it, while the man who hates his life in this world will keep it for eternal life" (John 12:25). Who owns your life?

Love is to be the air, the very breath, in which the Spirit-filled believer conducts his life; it is the garment (covering) he is to put on. Love is to be his consistent motivation at the root of all his actions. One's actions should reflect one's faith. Boys, you are to love God and others in such a way that it brings no moral condemnation upon you, so that you will reflect God's goodness to others. Love demands much of you. You are to love God's law, God's Word, and God's Son; you are to love God's hand of instruction, reproof, correction, and training. You are to love and endure your heavenly Father's tender discipline. It is expected that you will love and hold dear all of God's precious creation. Love demands that you be a man of righteous actions. What do your actions and behaviors say about your faith in the Lord Jesus? Are you a "doer of the Word" (James 1:22)? Love is accompanied by pragmatic and practical action; it leads, for example, to magnanimous giving (2 Corinthians 8:7) and genuine forgiveness (2 Corinthians 2:7). Is your faith producing Godly behavior?

God's goal in the work of divine love is the creation of the new man. The goal of love is for the man of Godly character to place his life in love and freedom, so as to serve his neighbor. Love is the foundation upon which Godly character is built. The man whose character is grounded in self-sacrificing love will naturally exhibit the following traits in some varying degree: joy, peace, patience, kindness, goodness, faithfulness, gentleness, and self-control.

We could spend the next several pages attempting to tell you what each of these eight descriptive qualities mean as derived from the original language. We could share with you the great theological themes that run through each of these characteristics; we could dissect each term and ask you to compare your life and character to each. The truth, however, is that these eight terms really do not need a lot of explanation. They are rather

67

self-explanatory. What we desire for you to know about being a man of integrity and character is simple. Ground your life in loving God with all your heart, with all your soul, and with all of your mind. Love God with everything you have, and then do all things—everything—to the glory of God. Do nothing in your life that is not done to the glory of God. From the spectacular to the common, do it all for the glory of God.

As you are loving God with all your heart, soul, and mind, discipline your life so that the natural outflow of that expressed love is revealed in your love for others. This revelation of love will expose itself through these eight qualities that are the fruit of the Spirit. You will be a man of joy and hope. You will be a whole person, a stable person, a man who is not at war with himself, God, or others. You will be a man of peace. Patience or endurance will illustrate your character.

As you love God and love others you will grow in kindness, gentleness, and goodness of the heart. You will mature in acts of goodness. Your character will become evident in your good deeds. You will excel in faithfulness. You will be trustworthy—a man driven by conviction. As a faithful person you will not only believe the truth; you will also work to ensure justice for others. Thoughts and words are not enough. Your life will reveal whether you are truly faithful. You will be characterized by a gentle or meek spirit. A meek demeanor is not to be confused with a weak manner; rather, gentleness communicates the idea of a controlled temperament or habit of the mind. Finally, you will be a man who practices self-control (temperance). It is the idea of "holding in hand the passions and desires of the flesh."

These eight qualities under the control of love are to be the basic building blocks of one's character, a character that is modeled on God's very own character. The fruit of the Spirit represent a very pragmatic and practical approach to living out the Great Commandment of Matthew 22:37-40. The character qualities of the fruit of the Spirit, however, are closely related to another kind of fruit—the results of one's life and ministry. What kind of influence on others and on the church does your character exert? Do the influences of your character build up and encourage or are they destructive? In Matthew 7:16-20, Jesus stated that every tree is known by the fruit it bears. How are you known? Are you bearing good or bad fruit?

RUNNING THE "GOOD RACE" & "FINISHING WELL"

Since Christ died to set us free from the restrictions and consequences of the law, our response is to stand firm and to not fall back into the old habits of the law and into sin. Stand firm in the work of Christ's saving grace; stand firm in your faith in Christ Jesus; stand firm in your resolve to run the good race, to persevere, and to finish well.

Perseverance is just a ten-dollar word for "sticking to it." Sticking with one thing in the face of distractions and difficulties is what perseverance and endurance is all about. You have a goal, a destination. You are going someplace. You have a God-given purpose. This is what sets the believer (you) apart from the unbeliever. Unbelievers see life as unpredictable, unreliable, and going nowhere. You have made a commitment to Jesus Christ, and He has made a commitment to you. He wants you to persevere until you reach the goal; in turn, He invests Himself in helping you accomplish this task. Jesus wants you to stick with one thing: running the race and finishing well; abiding in Him and producing good fruit; proving yourself a man and having integrity and Godly character.

But beware of the influence of others. Take heed of Paul's warning to the Galatians: "You were running a good race. Who cut in on you and kept you from obeying the truth?" (Galatians 5:7). We know it is a cliché, but you are the books you read, the "things" you listen to, the programs you watch, and the people you surround yourself with. Proverbs 23:7 says of the selfish man (the fool), "For as he thinks within himself, so he is." It is the truth of the old computer programmer's adage, "garbage in is garbage out." Boys, be careful of what you allow to influence your actions and behavior. Choose your books, your music, your TV, and your friends very carefully. Those "things" you meditate upon day and night are the "things" that you value. Friends can be a great encouragement or a great distraction. Do not allow your friends to be a pitfall to trap you in the ways of sin. Proverbs 4:13-17 instructs us to have a healthy skepticism concerning others.

Many proverbs point out that the "fruit of their ways" will be the consequences people will experience in this life. Faced with either choosing God's wisdom or persisting in rebellious independence, many decide to go it alone. Do not be like the crowd; be different. "All a man's ways seem right to him, but the Lord weighs the heart. To do what is right and just is more acceptable to the Lord than sacrifice" (Proverbs 21:2-3). You cannot "sit on the fence" of life; you cannot be a man of character and live for both fleshly pleasure and God's purposes. Why? Jesus gives us the reason in His Sermon on the Mount (Matthew 6:24), "No one can serve two masters; for either he will hate the one and love the other, or he will be devoted to one and despise the other." To whom do you belong?

In 1 Timothy 4:7, the apostle Paul encouraged Timothy to "discipline himself for the purpose of Godliness." In fact, Paul urged him to ignore all distractions and to set his aim upon Godliness as if nothing else existed. Such an undertaking requires discipline, effort, and perseverance. A Godly character is evident and visible for all to see, as is an ungodly character. This will not be easy. Developing and maintaining a Godly character takes daily effort. The apostle Peter would write, "Applying all diligence [effort], in your faith supply moral excellence, and in your moral excellence, knowledge, and in your knowledge, self-control, and in your self-control, perseverance, and in your perseverance, godliness, and in your godliness, brotherly kindness, and in your brotherly kindness, love" (2 Peter 1:5-7). Do you get the picture? It takes work, lots of work.

Look at what the apostle Paul says about running the race and finishing well. He admonishes the Corinthians to strive with a purpose. "Do you not know that in a race all the runners run, but only one gets the prize? Run in such a way as to get the prize" (1 Corinthians 9:24). How do you live your life? You live it "in such a way" so as to *win!* What is "such a way"? It is simply "walking in His ways." Paul instructs them that if they are going to accomplish this task, they will have to train themselves for the race. "Everyone who competes in the games goes into strict training" (1 Corinthians 9:25). Finally, He tells them that running to win takes effort and discipline. "Therefore I do not run like a man running aimlessly; I do not fight like a man beating the air. No, I beat my body and make it my slave so that after I have preached to others, I myself will not be disqualified for the prize" (1 Corinthians 9:24-27). In order to become a man of genuine, authentic, Christ-like character, you must discipline yourself; you must spend time with God—time in His Word and time in prayer. You must "walk in His ways." You must practice disciplined living.

DISCIPLINED LIVING

There were certain traits that David wanted Solomon to carry throughout his life. Boys (and dads), we are being very transparent in this book in that we are letting you into a part of our lives that we hold very personal. Both Andy and I pride ourselves on investing every fiber of our beings into your lives, the lives of our children. Does our world revolve around you? Even though it may seem like it at times, the answer is "No!" Being fathers is only a part of who we are. There are other roles we have that require our time and attention: husband, pastor, protector, and provider to name just a few. These roles, however, are arranged according to the priorities of our lives: our relationship with God, our relationship with our wives, our relationship with our children, and finally, our relationship with our churches. That is the way the priorities of our lives run, BUT when it comes to our roles as fathers, there is a very precise set of rules and priorities we follow, and there are a very precise set of outcomes that we expect. The same can be said of King David concerning the verses that we have anchored this work upon.

Boys, we are greatly concerned that there is not an overall working definition of what it means to be a man. We want you to have a clearly defined goal of what it means to be a man. A goal to which you can aim, and when you reach it other men, us included, will be able to affirm and recognize that you have indeed become a man—a man who has fully comprehended and reached that goal. The charge that David gave to Solomon—keep God's ways, His commandments, statutes, ordinances, and testimonies—is the blueprint for determining what true manhood looks like. It is the goal to which we want you to aim. It is the mark by which all will know that you are truly a man.

Think about this: As Solomon cultivated those attributes in his own life, his father knew that his son would grow into a man who would follow God. David's plan was solid. The Bible, however, tells us that Solomon failed at following his father's words; and outside of completing God's temple, making a famous decision about cutting a baby in half, and writing down a few words of wisdom, Solomon did not do much of anything else worth remembering. Actually, in the end, Solomon, for all of his wisdom and early promise, failed to follow his own advice and turned away from the God of his fathers. Solomon's life was quite a letdown from the lofty expectations that his father laid before him. We can only trust God for the results of the application and fruition of our working definition of manhood in your lives. Such trust is not an easy out or an excuse for us to be lazy in our approach to fatherhood. If we fail, if you end up failing—may it not be because we did not take our role as father seriously. We pray for God's strength to empower us to mold you into men who follow God's ways.

When we go "the way of all the earth," we want to leave behind sons who understand that God-following men are disciplined, gentle, generous, and faithful. That is it. There is the blueprint. This is our working definition of manhood—disciplined, gentle, generous, and faithful. Sounds easy enough, does is not? The God-following man is disciplined, gentle, generous, and faithful. If we could see into your future and catch a glimpse of you at the end of your life, regardless of your education, your economic standings, or your position, if we were to see that you were men who were known for these four qualities, then we would be very well pleased with you. We could "go the way of all the earth" with a smile on our face. Allow us to tell you why by taking each one of these characteristics one at a time, starting with discipline. We pray that you will learn to be disciplined with your time, love, hope, and attitudes.

DISCIPLINED WITH YOUR TIME

It has been said that there are two things you can never produce more of: more land and more time. The reason is simple; no one is making any more of them. The value of land hardly ever decreases, because there is only so much on the earth. God is not making any more. And time is pretty much the same way. You only have twenty-four hours in a day, seven days a week, and 365 days in a given year. There is only so much time. Boys, will you be wise enough to invest your time in things that really matter? Will you be disciplined enough to enjoy your time and use each and every second of it to truly live and build the kingdom of God, or will you be interested in building your own kingdom?

We pray that you use what time you are given to be builders of God's kingdom. May you never get caught up in the rat race of building a career or fretting over the details of life that have no eternal significance. Whether it is your homework or keeping the oil in your vehicle changed, live your life to the fullest; stay busy and productive, but do not waste the valuable, precious time that God has given you on worrying over the details. Remember what Jesus said in Matthew 6:34, "So do not worry about tomorrow; for tomorrow will care for itself. Each day has enough trouble of its own." What significance do food, drink, and clothes have in the eternal scheme of life? Those are just the details. Now, do not misunderstand us. There will be times when you will be called upon to pay attention to the details. There is no shame in working hard to provide the essentials of food, housing, and clothing for your family, but what we are warning you against is the futility of worrying over such things. Synchronize your watch to run on God's time, and all the things you need will be added to your life.

DISCIPLINED IN YOUR LOVE

We want you to become disciplined in the area of love. Boys, listen to Clay's testimony concerning this vital area of your lives.

Aslan and Haddon, your mother and I are so thankful to have been brought up in the families God gave us. Both of us grew up in homes where our parents had their wedding day pictures taken in black and white; in other words, they got married a long time ago and stayed together for a very long time. Both your mother and I were raised in wonderful loving homes; it simply astonishes and amazes us how God used our parents (and our families) to foster the love for family that we have.

That same love for family has carried over into each of your lives. We know that you will never doubt the love that we have for your mothers, the love that your mothers have for us, the love we share for each of you, and the love you share for us. We pray that the love we learned from our parents—the love that you are seeing in our homes—will ultimately be carried over into your future homes, your future families. There have been many nights that we, your parents, have prayed for your future wives, our future daughter in-laws. We pray that you find and marry a Godly woman.

All of this is to say that Andy and I want you to be disciplined in the area of honoring your family as well as the commitments you will make to your future bride and to your children. We also want you to be disciplined in the practice of that love. We want you to know the difference between love and lust, love and like, dating and courting. We want you to be distinctive in how you treat the opposite gender. We want you to be gentlemen, treating each person with the respect that is due them for simply having been made in the image of God—especially those of the opposite sex. Boys, we expect you to not only act like gentlemen; we expect you to be gentlemen. What does it mean to be a gentleman? What does it look like?

- It is when Haddon holds the door for a lady when we are in town.
- It is when Duncan opens the car door for his mother or his sister.
- It is having the expectation that Aslan will walk on the outside (street side) when he is escorting his mother in town.
- It is teaching Duncan to rise when a woman comes to the table.

The list could go on and on. These are not mere courtesies; love expressed via action is the bedrock, the foundation of being a disciplined man. A gentleman will value the honor and the reputation of a young lady. Being a gentleman in our current culture is a dead idea, an extinct concept. We want you to be men who stand against the culture; we want you to be gentlemen.

DISCIPLINED WITH YOUR HOPE

Boys, our desire is that you will understand that since you are part of a covenant home—that is, your mother and father are believers and followers of the Lord Jesus Christ—you have something in which to place your hope. As a Christian, you have a hope that is simply indefinable in terms that an unbeliever could understand. Romans 8:22-25 speaks to hoping in something that cannot be seen by human eyes. Our deepest prayer is that you will place your hope not in the words of a doctor, nor in aspirations for higher education, but rather in the new Earth that is promised in Revelation 21. Whatever life throws at you or wherever life takes you, we pray that your focus remains on the world that is to come and on the One that will ultimately make all things new.

DISCIPLINED IN YOUR ATTITUDES

What kind of attitude toward God are you taking with you when you leave our house to go to school, to church, to the park, to the ball field, to the movies, to the arcade, to the mall, to your friend's house, or anywhere? Are you leaving with an attitude of appreciation and service? We ponder these same thoughts concerning your attitude toward God and the things of God when you finally leave home to start your own life. Will you continue to follow God when you no longer have to?

I (Clay) recall my very first Sunday of independent living at college. It never occurred to me that I could choose to not go to church. I just went to First Baptist Church in Clinton, Mississippi. I am not bragging. In fact, if there is anyone to brag on, it would be my folks—your grandparents. I can honestly say that from nine months before I was born, I was shown the attractiveness of Christ. Did I ever wish to stay home and watch Flipper on Sunday mornings? You bet, but because of those earliest attitude adjustments, I have never waned too far from the active body of believers known as the church.

Boys, our attitude toward God—the love we have for Him, for His Son, Jesus, and His Church—is the reason why we attend church each Sunday. We do not attend because a group of people pays us to be there as ministers. We go to church because we love God, we love His people, and we love to obey His Word. Understand this one very simple fact: As long as we have breath in our lungs and any amount of influence over you, you will be found worshiping with a Bible-believing church. We do not know a lot, but what we do know, we know a lot about. We know church trends. We know church folks. We know that if a young man is not active in church in his teens, then he will not be active in his twenties; if not in his twenties, forget his thirties. Do you get the picture?

We do not want you to have to "rededicate" your lives to Christ at some later point because you went astray during some earlier stage of life. We want you to sell out completely for Christ and never look back with regret; we want you to be disciplined in your attitude toward following God all the days of your life. We believe that the right attitude, if placed in a child's life and reinforced throughout his life, will guarantee that there is never a need to rededicate anything.

WALKING IN HIS WAYS

We are trying to give you a working definition of what manhood is all about, and as you progress through life, it will be our pleasure to mark the occasions that prove to you that you are getting closer to the goal. Finally, there will come a day when we will prayerfully turn you loose on the world with something more than just a diploma or a degree or a new wife by which you can define manhood. We will turn you loose to be men molded in the image of 1 Kings 2:2-3—men who are disciplined with their time, love, hope, and attitude.

There are two truths that we want you to take away from us on that day when you finally become men. Both are scripturally based.

#1—The results of disciplined living
(Proverbs 23:15-16)

My son, if your heart is wise, my own heart also will be glad; and my inmost being will rejoice when your lips speak what is right.

If we, as your dads, are willing to go to such great lengths to invest ourselves in your lives, then please understand that by reaching the end result and achieving this definition of manhood, you will make your fathers glad.

To know that your hearts are wise = Our hearts will be glad.
Our hearts will rejoice = To hear your lips speak what is right.

Our hearts will be glad and the innermost parts of our beings will rejoice. This is not a self-given high-five or a pat on the back. We gladly surrender the honor to the God that created in you, the same love for Him and His word as He did in our own lives. The greatest legacy that you, our sons, can give us is to not let the work stop with you. Solomon took the ball from his father and dropped it. Boys, we pray that you will take what we are giving to you and run with it.

#2—The strength for disciplined living
(2 Peter 1:3-5)

Blessed be the God and Father of our Lord Jesus Christ, who according to His great mercy has caused us to be born again to a living hope through the resurrection of Jesus Christ from the dead, to obtain an inheritance which is imperishable and undefiled and will not fade away, reserved in heaven for you, who are protected by the power of God through faith for a salvation ready to be revealed in the last time.

You can do this! The power source is already there. It is not as though you are the little engine that continually has to repeat, "I think I can, I think I can." Your life is to be lead by the motto, "I know He did, I know He did." You have been given something that worldly standards cannot match—an inheritance from God Himself, and not just any inheritance, but one that is imperishable, undefiled, will not fade away, reserved in heaven, and protected!

LIFE APPLICATION QUESTIONS:
CHAPTER 3

1) What does the following old proverb mean?
   "Character is who you are when nobody is looking."
   In your own words, restate this proverb.
2) Here are a few Biblical characters. Name one character flaw that each man possessed.

David

Moses

Peter

After discussing these men and their respective failures, how do you feel concerning your own spiritual walk?

3) John Piper has said, "It's not that I do bad things. I am bad." What is the difference between doing bad and being bad? What is the only way to "fix" our bad problem?

HELPFUL HINT

Let your child see you doing one of the following within the next few days:

- Reading your Bible
- Holding your spouse's hand in public
- Serving in some way at church

END NOTES

Anthony, Michael. 2001. *Introducing Christian Education.* Grand Rapids, MI: Baker Academic.

Blackaby, Henry and Tom Blackaby. 1998. *The Man God Uses.* Nashville, TN: LifeWay Press.

Cole, Edwin Louis. 1992. *Real Man.* Nashville, TN: Thomas Nelson Publishers.

Erickson, Millard J. 1992. *Introducing Christian Doctrine*. Grand Rapids, MI: Baker Academic.

Fung, Ronald Y. K. 1998. *The Epistle to the Galatians, NICNT*. Grand Rapids, MI: Eerdmans.

Grudem, Wayne. 1994. *Systematic Theology*. Grand Rapids, MI: Zondervan.

Longnecker, Richard N. 1990. *Galatians*. Dallas, TX: Word Books Publishers.

Andy's son, Duncan, catching frogs

CHAPTER FOUR

Keep His Commandments—God Honors Obedience

G oing to town was a big deal when I was growing up. When the Gowins family went to town, it almost always meant that we would be stopping by the local drug store. It seemed like we were always getting medicine for somebody in the family. The best thing about the drug store was that they had two aisles in the back corner of the store loaded down with toys—cars, dolls, action figures, balls, games. To a five-year-old it was as if Christmas had come early. I can remember roaming up and down those aisles looking at everything and wanting everything. I can recall one afternoon very well.

There are those days that happen in your life; they are good days, but they are unremarkable days—days that you will not remember. But then there are those days that will leave their mark on you for the rest of your life. It was one of those days that I will never forget and has shaped my life ever since. It was late in the afternoon when Mom whipped into the parking lot at Pat's Drug Store. Mr. Pat was the pharmacist and owner of the drug store. As we rushed in, Mom headed for the pharmacy counter, and I headed for the back corner of the store—toys! It did not take me very long; within minutes I was searching through the toys, looking for any new arrivals since my last visit. That is when I saw it. "It" was the coolest-looking miniature motorized car I had ever seen. As I picked it up in its display box and began to investigate every panel of the box, the box lid came open.

Peering inside the box, I could see the car. I knew that we could not afford this toy and I knew it would be a wasted effort to even ask; but I really wanted this car. That is when I saw the folded tri-fold advertisement for not only this car, but several other miniature motorized vehicles, in the box behind the car, and I wanted it. Now, I knew that stealing was wrong, and there was no way I would ever be able to get the car out of the store and back to the house without my mom discovering my "new" toy. Certainly no one would miss the folded advertisement of all those cool cars and trucks. It was not as if it was the actual car itself, and advertisements were for looking at anyway. It would not really be stealing. With my heart racing and with a quick look around the back corner of the store, I reached in the box, took out the advertisement, crammed it into the front pocket of my jeans, and walked out of the store a few minutes later following my mom. Relief—I made it and no one was the wiser. No one knew. No one saw me.

But, someone did see me; someone did know; someone very wise was onto me. Boys, there is always One who sees and knows everything, and He delights in "chastising those He loves" (Hebrews 12:6). By the time we got home that evening, I had forgotten all about the advertisement that I just had to have crammed in the front pocket of my jeans; but it did not go unnoticed by my mom. She found it that night while she was doing the laundry. The next morning at breakfast, Mom served me a plate of pancakes stacked tall, syrup and butter on the side, a big glass of ice-cold milk, and a straightened-out, once-crumpled, folded tri-fold advertisement for miniature motorized cars and trucks! My secret crime was no longer a secret.

A moment of greed, of lust, and of covetousness resulted in a foolish decision and an act of disobedience. I had sinned against God, God's law, and my parents. After confessing my crime to both my mom and dad, I was driven back to Pat's Drug Store and was made to go inside (alone), confess my actions to Mr. Pat, ask for forgiveness, and accept whatever consequences he thought appropriate. I was all of five years old. That was one of those days that left its mark on me forever.

David's charge to his son Solomon to "be strong, show yourself a man, and observe what the Lord your God requires: Walk in his ways, and keep his decrees and commands, his laws and requirements..." (1 Kings 2:1-3), is all about obedience. Walking in God's way, being a young man of character and integrity, whose character is defined by the fruit of the Spirit demands obedience to God's laws—His commandments. We know what you are thinking, "What? I've got to obey all ten of the commandments?" No! You do not have to obey all ten. You have got to obey *all* of God's commandments, and there are more than just the Ten Commandments. You are responsible for knowing and living each and every commandment given by God through His Holy Spirit that we find in His self-revelation—the Bible. However, there is no way we can discuss every one of them; so, we are going to focus on just the big ten.

Without doubt, the Ten Commandments are the most famous rules ever given. Both Christians and non-Christians have some knowledge and/or awareness of them, and could probably even quote at least one or two of them. These ten rules represent the most basic of God's laws, summarizing the most common acts of human disobedience, but they are not an exhaustive list of every possible transgression. These ten rules are God's standards for how we are to live right with Him, according to Deuteronomy 5:6-21. To obey them is to obey God. They were purposefully designed to lead Israel (and us) to a life of practical holiness. The Ten Commandments reveal the very nature of God and His plan for how we are to live.

As is always important to the New Testament Church and Christians, it is vital to examine any Old Testament teaching in view of what the New Testament reveals about it. Does the New Testament have anything to add to the Ten Commandments? You had better believe it. In His Sermon on the Mount, Jesus explained that God was not merely giving us a set of rules. He was, in fact, telling each of us what our hearts should be like. In other words, it is not enough in the eyes of God for His people to simply obey the rules. God desires our obedience to be motivated by our deep love for Him and everything about Him: "You shall love the Lord your God with all your heart, all your mind, and all your strength" (Matthew 22:37). It is possible to obey all Ten Commandments and still not love God. Boys, the Lord your God wants you to obey Him simply because you love Him: "If anyone loves me, he will obey my teaching" (John 14:23).

Ah, the questions we can hear. "But Dad, I thought that was then and this is now? Wasn't the law done away with when Jesus died on the cross? You have always taught me, my Sunday school teachers have taught me, and the preacher shouts it out each week that my salvation is by the grace of God alone. Why should I obey the Ten Commandments?" Those are great questions, and they demand even greater answers. The simple answer is because God has said so! The more complicated answer, however, is because the law was never intended to save anyone. Its function is still the same today as it was when the very finger of God wrote it down on the two stone tablets that Moses carried down from the Mountain of God. In Galatians 2:15-16, the apostle Paul informs us that the law can never make us acceptable to God. The law was given to mankind to guard us from sinning (disobeying) against God and one another. It was given so that we might know when we have done wrong; it convicts us of our disobedience. Remember, the concept of being convicted explicitly implies that the person who is being convicted has been found guilty of a crime. There is no degree to the level or intensity of this person's guilt. It is simply the cold hard fact that they are guilty. They are not innocent. The law declares you guilty before a holy God. The consequence of your guilt demands your separation from God. The sentence, the punishment, for disobedience is banishment to hell, a place of eternal darkness (Jesus, the light of the world, is not there), a place of weeping and the gnashing of teeth (Matthew 25:28). Oh, but praise God for the cross!

While it is true that the law can never save, its convicting nature drives us to trust in the supremacy and sufficiency of Christ Jesus. The law, those Ten Commandments, point the way to Jesus, who is "the Way, the Truth, and the Life" by which no one can enter into the presence of the Father lest they enter through Him—the Christ. If you want to live a life that honors God, then practice the greatest of the commandments—love God with all your heart, mind, and strength—and then practice that love by loving others. If you want to know how to love God and others in such a way, the Ten Commandments are the best place to start. A word of caution, however. If you are not keeping the Ten Commandments, do not fool yourself; you have not yet mastered the basic expectations of the Christian life. Remember, these commandments are to govern your actions, but also, more importantly, your attitudes.

HOW TO LOVE GOD

When Jesus answered the Scribes as to which commandment was the greatest, the most important, and the most significant of all, He was simply summarizing the first four of the Ten Commandments (Exodus 20:1-11).

- I am the Lord your God, who brought you out of Egypt, out of the land of slavery. You shall have no other gods before me.
- You shall not make for yourself an idol in the form of anything in heaven above or on the earth beneath or in the waters below.
- You shall not misuse the name of the Lord your God.
- Remember the Sabbath day by keeping it holy.

As well as, emphasizing the great Shema of Israel found in Deuteronomy 6:4-6:

Hear, O Israel: The Lord our God, the Lord is one. Love the Lord your God with all your heart and with all your soul and with all your strength. These commandments that I give you today are to be upon your hearts.

Boys, we want you to know these commandments. Know them in your mind (to memorize them), know them in your heart (to believe in them), and know them in your life (to practice them). Let us take a quick look at what it means to love God.

Before we start talking about these first four commandments, we want to ask you a question. Why do you think people—church people, people who claim to be believers and followers of the Lord Jesus Christ—why do they not live lives that are visibly, radically, and significantly different from those who do not believe and/or are not followers of Jesus? The local church is full of men, women, boys, girls, moms, dads, grandfathers, and grandmothers who look like, smell like, and act like those in our communities who are unchurched and do not have a relationship with God. The answer to the question breaks our hearts; church folks are not visibly different in their actions and attitudes from their unchurched counterparts because they simply do not understand who God really is.

HOW TO RESPECT GOD

Even though we know that there is only one God, sometimes the way we live tells a different story. God is the Creator and Lord of the universe; He is God alone—the one and only God. He deserves your first loyalty. Put God first and give Him your total devotion. God is always to be your highest priority. Let nothing or no one take first place in your heart over God. The Bible states that God is a jealous God (Exodus 20:5). The concept of "the jealous God" is a direct reference to the marital covenant agreement that a man is to have with his wife. God is comparing His relationship with His followers to the fidelity that ought to be present in the marriage relationship between a husband and a wife. Allow us to illustrate this for you. It is not wrong for us to make the bold statement that we are jealous for your mothers, our wives. We are jealous for 100% of our wife's attention; 100% of her love; 100% of her devotion. We will not accept anything less. We will not share her with another man. Neither Clay nor I will tolerate any competition for the affection or favor of our wives. This is exactly how God feels, "Thou shall not have any other gods before me" (Exodus 20:3).

A god is anything a person allows to rule his or her life. Other gods could include: deities of other religions, superstitions, horoscopes, money, possessions, career, personal comfort, family, friends, addictions, fame, power, security, romance, sex, church, extreme patriotism—anything that comes before God. When your loyalty is divided, you have elevated something else into God's rightful place. Watch over your heart that you allow nothing to become more important to you than pleasing God.

In the First Commandment, God establishes His identity as the sovereign Lord, the supreme God, the Alpha and the Omega. By delivering the children of Israel from the bondage of Egyptian slavery, the Lord God demonstrated His absolute superiority over all the false gods of Egypt. Who is His rival; who can rebut the

Word of God; who can refuse the sovereign and holy one?

God's Word says, "Train up a child in the way he should go; and when he is old, he will not depart from it" (Proverbs 22:6). Boys, we pray that we have taught you the truth of the First Commandment; we pray that you have paid attention; we pray that you know that we love God first and foremost; and our prayer is that you love Him in the same way. If you truly love God, then you will give Him the respect He deserves. True love for God always translates into obedience to Him.

HOW TO KNOW GOD

The Second Commandment is really a continuation and a deepening in our understanding of the First Commandment. While it is true that our God is just, loving, and long-suffering, He is God and He is holy! By His very nature He cannot tolerate sin; He will not tolerate idols in our hearts. There is room for only one master in our lives, and God alone holds the rights to that position. Simply stated, we become like the "thing" we worship.

We know what you are thinking. Of course, you are technically correct. We are not in the business of crafting idols and/or images of false gods. In fact, the idea is almost laughable, except for the fact that we have made idols of many things in our lives. Who can compare to God? There is no one. An idol is a material thing, a created thing. It is an object created by the imagination and hands of humanity. No idol can represent the invisible, spiritual God. What can you compare God to or with? There is only one God, and His throne only seats one. He is not a part-time king. He is God! Do not forget, He is a jealous

God and demands your attention and your worship twenty-four hours a day, seven days a week. You have no right to worship anything or anybody but Him.

Anything you love more than God, anything you fear more than God, anything you serve more than God, anything you value more than God—that is your god. We have made gods of ourselves, our families, our jobs, and even our pursuit of pleasure. Whatever your heart embraces and regards as vital, that thing is your god. Put your faith in God and God alone. Know who God is and choose to worship Him. Idol worship is worshiping or serving anything in the place of God. Love God by devoting yourself to Him completely. Just as God is a jealous God, we want you to be a jealous follower of Jesus Christ.

How to treat God

Loving God with all of your heart, mind, and soul not only requires that you know who He is and that you place Him first in your life, it also means that you must understand that God is worthy to be worshiped and He is to be worshiped at all times. This is the reality of the Third Commandment. We are commanded to respect the name of the Lord. We are not to use it in vain. Vanity translates "meaningless, empty of content; erratic, worthless; nonproductive." It is the idea of lifting up something emptily or without intent.

This commandment encompasses so much more than just simple profanity or cursing. There is no doubt that profanity is not acceptable. It is vulgar and takes that which is holy and set apart and makes it common and ordinary. Cursing reveals a simple mind attempting to communicate. The use of foul language exposes a wicked heart (Matthew 12:34) (Rogers, 1996, p. 60). Besides, if you understand the concept of cursing, taking God's name in vain (as a compound curse-word), you understand that it only demonstrates one's ignorance. In order to curse something or someone, you must possess power and authority over that something or that someone. If God is who He claims to be (and we have no reason to doubt His claim), who has power or authority over Him? Is not that the whole point of the first two commandments? Therefore, taking God's name in vain is a pointless and excuseless sin. It is impossible to curse God! Taking His name in vain is an act of disobedience that only serves to illustrate one's contempt for the holy God—the Creator of the heavens above and the earth below. Oh, how ignorant we can be of the one we worship.

As long as we are talking about profanity, boys, allow us to warn you against the fallacy of secondhand swearing. What is secondhand swearing? It is the substitution of non-swear words, non-profanity, to communicate a profane thought. Such words as gosh, darn, dang, shoot, jeez or any other word that you would use in place of a socially unacceptable curse word is secondhand profanity. We have been commanded to not take the name of our Lord God in vain; while we refer to Him as God, God is not His name. He identified Himself to Moses as "the God of Abraham, Isaac, and Joseph...the I AM" (Exodus 3:6). The Jewish people were so careful to follow this commandment that they would not even spell His name, or speak His name. Instead they referred to Him as Lord. We are not even for certain that the name Yahweh is His name, although we are certain that it is a reference to Him. What we are trying to say is that whether you call Him: Lord, Yahweh, Jehovah, God, Jesus, gosh, jeez, or the I AM, you are using all of these names to refer to the Almighty God, the Creator, and the Father of our Lord Jesus Christ.

Pay careful attention, boys—any word can be abused and become secondhand profanity. When my sister and I (Andy) were very young (between the ages of three and five), we cursed like sailors, or so I am told. You see, whenever we got mad, upset, or wanted to communicate our displeasure, we would say mean and hateful things using the names of convenient stores and grocery stores. Mom and Dad thought it was funny and cute, until they realized what was going on. We were swearing. "Go to (insert the name of your favorite grocery store)," or just shout out the name of your favorite convenient store in frustration. Jesus stated in the gospels that it is not what we put in our mouths that makes us dirty and unclean; it is what comes out of our mouths (our words) that reveals the condition (the attitude) of our hearts that makes us dirty and unclean (Matthew 15:18). Secondhand swearing is just as wicked, pointless, and sinful as using the real words. Stay away and guard your witness from even the hint of evil. Do not use secondhand profanity.

As we have already shared with you, this commandment is not primarily concerned with the act of swearing. Unfortunately, that is as far as most of us go with it. But, as we have already shared with you, there are many other ways to lift the name of God up emptily, to take the name of God in vain. One such way is simply to use it foolishly, thoughtlessly, or trivially. Boys, do not use the name of your God carelessly or lightly. Such empty talk is much more common than simple profanity. The apostle Paul warns against useless talk in Ephesians 5:3-6. What is foolish or jesting speech? It is the thoughtless, superficial, frivolous manner in which we so easily include the holy name of God in our common everyday speech. Only use God's name if you are serious. Be careful to guard against such trivial phrases as "Oh, Lord," or "Oh, my God."

Another way in which you can take the name of your God in vain is to use it dishonestly. Be careful not to be hypocritical when you use the name of God. When you use God's name in a way that is not truthful or righteous, you are being deceitful about the nature and the person of God. "I would never do that, Dad," you proclaim. Really? Have you ever "sworn to God"? What about when you pray; do you just add the name of Jesus onto the end because that is the way you pray, or are you presenting your praises, petitions, and requests to God through Christ Jesus, your High Priest, who intercedes upon your behalf before God the Father? When you lift up your voice in song during weekly worship, are you singing and praising with all your heart or are you lifting up empty praises in the name of your God? When you hear others using God's name in vain, what assumption do you make about their view of God? Do not let others have such a view of you.

Taking God's name in vain is abusing the name of God. Anything that diminishes the value of God's name is abusing His name. Do not mock God. Show Him the fearful reverence and respect that He deserves instead of the contempt of disrespecting His name. Do not misrepresent Him; give God the absolute respect He deserves. He is God! Do not slander the character of God or His name by justifying sinful, disobedient, and unrighteousness acts. Professing to be a follower of Jesus Christ, yet living as if God has no power to help you, communicates to others that God is less than He claims to be, that He is powerless over sin. Do not mock God; protect His holy name and His reputation.

HOW TO EXPERIENCE GOD

The Fourth Commandment insists upon a day of rest—a day that is set aside as a holy day, a day upon which the people of God are to stop working so that they can focus together as a community of believers on a regular basis. The Lord your God rested upon the seventh day, setting the example of what He expects of mankind—the Sabbath as a day of rest and a day of worship. This is why God created the Sabbath. While the saints of the Old Testament celebrated the Sabbath on the last day of the week, the early New Testament church celebrated God's day on Sunday, the first day of the week, in honor of the day Jesus was raised from the dead.

The Sabbath was (and is) God's gift given to His chosen people, the Israelites, and then to the church. It is a day of rest after six days of labor. In Mark 2:27, Jesus states that "The Sabbath was made for man, and not man for the Sabbath." It is a holy day that has been set apart for a specific purpose.

Make worship on Sunday your highest weekly priority. Duncan, early in our dating relationship, your mom and I made a "once-and-for-all" decision. We decided that we would attend worship by going to church on Sunday mornings, Sunday nights, and Wednesday nights. We determined to be part of weekly corporate worship. No longer would we have to wake up on Sunday morning or come in from class (we were in college at the time) on Wednesday nights and struggle with the question of whether or not we were going to go to church. That decision had already been made. Make worship on Sunday your highest weekly priority.

You should not only worship on this day, but you should also rest. God values rest, spiritual refreshment, and time for His people to worship Him. Sunday is not a day to catch up on your chores. It is not a day to mow the yard. It is not a day to go into work and get ahead. It is to be a day of rest. Without physical rest, your body can become tired, worn down, and unproductive; without regular spiritual refreshment, your relationship with God can become tired, worn down, and unproductive. It is possible to have a rested physical body and still have a restless mind and spirit. To rest is to be fulfilled. Thus, the very definition of rest for the Christian is the worship of God. To be fulfilled in God, this is what you were made for. Your fulfillment is found in your worship of God. The Sabbath day of rest is an opportunity for you to renew your relationship with God and refocus on Him by honoring Him in your worship. Sunday is a day to be spent with family and friends celebrating what the Lord your God is doing in your life and the lives of those you love. As a believer in the Living God, Sunday ought to be the happiest day of your week.

The Sabbath day of rest allows you a regular time of reflection to check your priorities. Stop and evaluate the way you are living; make the necessary changes in your attitude so that you can "love the Lord your God with all your heart, mind, and soul." Keep the Sabbath holy; set it aside and dedicate it to the Lord your God.

Duncan, it is late Sunday evening as I sit here and type these thoughts. I have had one of the best times of my life tonight with you. Tonight our church hosted a youth evangelism rally and Mom, Sis, you, and I volunteered our time to meet and greet the four or five hundred area youth that came. While all of that was very exciting, what was most exciting to me was watching you worship God. Wow! As the worship leader and praise band led us to the very throne of heaven, I could hear your little eight-year-old voice singing at the top of your lungs. I watched as your body shook and squirmed as you wanted to let loose and just worship God the way He had created you to worship Him. I could feel the electricity of the moment as we shouted out "Holy! Holy! Holy! Hallelujah He reigns!" I do not believe that I will ever forget this night. This is what it is all about. This is what you were created for; this is what I want for you! This is what it means to be a follower and a believer of the Lord Jesus Christ.

Boys, this may sound completely corny, but it is completely true: We love you. We only want what is best for you; we want you to be successful in life and to have true joy. This is where it is found. It is only when you are in the center of God's majestic presence that you can have true joy and true success. The best and most loving gift we could ever give you is teaching you, leading you, and assisting you to walk daily in the presence of the Living God. You will never be truly able to walk in His presence and worship Him in holy energetic spirit-filled reverence if you do not put these first four commandments to work in your life.

To love Him is to worship Him and Him alone. It is to pledge your undying and unswerving loyalty to God Almighty. To devote yourself to Him means that you will not allow any created thing to come between you and God. Such a devotion demands that you approach God daily with clean hands and a pure heart, constantly casting down the idols of this life that seek to distract you from His perfect presence. To know Him demands that you respect Him! When you see God for who He is, what He is capable of, and how much He loves you, your only response can be to fall down on your knees and praise Him; praise Him with holy lips, recounting His glorious character. But how can you declare His character if you lift His holy name up in emptiness, vanity? Guard the name of your God! He is your Lord; He is your King! To praise Him requires that we set aside time for Him and Him alone. Boys, following these first four commandments will always allow you the opportunity to worship the Lord your God in spirit and in truth. As they permeate every area of your life, you will be able to lift up holy hands and with a loud voice cry out those wonderful words, "Holy! Holy! Holy! Hallelujah He reigns!"

HOW TO TREAT OTHERS

There is so much more we would like to share with you about loving God with all of your heart, all of your mind, and all of your soul; but alas, much of what we would love to share with

101

you, you will just have to learn it on your own. This we can promise you, however; if you will commit yourself to loving God by making Him your number one priority in life by worshiping Him and Him alone, by treating Him with the respect and reverence that Almighty God deserves, and by setting time aside both daily and weekly to spend with Him, you will do well in life. The Old Testament speaks of this concept of loving God in terms of fearing Him. Proverbs 1:7 states that "The fear of the Lord is the beginning of knowledge or wisdom." We want you to fear God; God the creator of heaven and earth, who with a spoken word caused all of creation to come into being; God the Holy One, whose very character separates Him from sinful humanity; God the Eternal Judge, who will one day pour out His wrath on those who decided to defy Him. He is to be greatly feared! But you can only truly begin to understand the great miracle and work of the cross, His grace, and His mercy only when you truly understand the very character of God and what His character demands of us. Only when you fear Him in light of His character can you truly love Him.

It is interesting to note that when He was asked to define and describe which of the commandments was the greatest, Jesus summarized all of the commandments in two statements: loving God with all of your being, and loving your neighbor even as you love yourself. If you proclaim to love God, there had better be evidence in your life and relationships with others that expresses the love of God through you to your fellow man. In other words, if you do not show love and kindness to others, it is questionable as to whether or not you truly love God. While the first four commandments deal exclusively with your relationship with and toward God, the last six commandments deal with how you will relate to your neighbors.

Remember Jesus' own words, "If you love me, you will keep my commandments" (John 14:15), and let us not forget God's own words that obedience is more desired, better, than sacrifice (Hosea 6:6). The Lord honors obedience and obedience demands your attention to these last six commandments.

How to treat your family

"Honor your father and mother" (Exodus 20:12). God wants all people to respect and honor those He has placed in authority. The first and perhaps primary institution in which God has vested authority is the family. This is not a suggestion or a best practice; it is a commandment. You have been commanded to treat your parents with respect, regardless of what your situation may be. Why? This commandment is significant because the family is the foundational unit of any and every society.

The family is so important in God's divine plan that the Fifth Commandment is the first, and only, of God's Ten Commandments that comes with a direct promise attached to it (Exodus 20:12; Ephesians 6:2). God has given you a family for living with, for protecting you as well as for teaching you. Showing respect to your family is an act of obedience to God rather than an act of submission to your family. You are treating them as Christ would.

Our goal is to be Godly fathers, worthy of your respect and honor, setting before you a Godly example. Your goal should be to be Godly sons, growing in the wisdom of the Lord, learning valuable life lessons from our experiences, aspiring to someday be a Godly father (if the Lord so leads) so that you can set your own Godly example. We do believe in the principle of Proverbs 22:6. We are training you in the way you should go, and we are claiming the promise that you will not easily depart from that path. Yes! But, we also know that you have a will of your own, and that your faith must be your faith. You are responsible for your own actions, attitudes, and decisions. Your actions speak much louder than your words; this is especially true concerning how you act and behave in the home. "Decide this day who you will serve."

HOW TO TREAT YOURSELF

While the Sixth Commandment is clearly addressing the act of murder, we want to use this commandment to talk to you about practicing self-control. It is not really that much of a stretch. In his Sermon on the Mount, Jesus uses this commandment to bring fresh understanding to the intent of the law (Matthew 5:21-26). Jesus affirms that murder is evil and wrong, but He takes it one step further; He goes to the root or the cause of murder—anger. Anyone who harbors anger in his heart toward another, according to Jesus, is guilty of murder. Everyone is guilty of violating the Sixth Commandment. While few people ever reach the point of actually murdering someone, all of us have experienced anger, and at the root of every murder there is an angry attitude.

The apostle Paul had much to say about anger and self-control.

In Ephesians 5:26-27 he states, "In your anger do not sin: Do not let the sun go down while you are still angry, and give the devil a foothold." When you are angry, when you are out of control, you are a fertile playground for your enemy, the devil. Paul goes on to tell his readers to "Get rid of all bitterness, rage, and anger, brawling and slander, along with every form of malice. Be kind and compassionate to one another, forgiving each other, just as in Christ God forgave you" (Ephesians 5:31-32). How do you guard against anger? You must have a compassionate and forgiving character. This is much easier said than done, but so is living the Christian lifestyle.

It takes self-control, guided by the Holy Spirit, to be obedient in following this commandment. Do not pollute your body, your spirit, your emotions, or your mind with unrighteous and unholy anger. Your body is the temple of God's Holy and Living Spirit. Stay in control of yourself or better yet, stay under the control of Christ through His Holy Spirit. Do not let the lusts of the flesh control you: food addictions, pornography, or sexual addictions; do not pollute your body with drugs, alcohol, or tobacco; and do not allow unwholesome thoughts that are displeasing to God to detract you from being qualified to serve the Master. Once again in Ephesians, the apostle Paul gives us some of the best advice we will ever receive in terms of practicing self-control: "Be very careful, then, how you live...making the most of every opportunity...understand what the Lord's will is...Do not get drunk on wine...instead, be filled with the Spirit" (Ephesians 5:15-18). Be filled with the Spirit and practice self-control.

HOW TO TREAT YOUR HEART

Wow! Now it is time for "the sex talk." We can remember how embarrassing it was when our dads had this talk with us; we do not want you to be embarrassed. In fact, let us start off by saying that the act of sex is GREAT and even more importantly it is GOOD. God gave mankind this wonderful expression of intimacy and love, and it was a perfect gift; however, sin and man's depraved mind and lusts have corrupted God's perfect gift. Just as God wants you to worship Him and only Him, just as God has commanded you to honor and respect your parents, just as God expects you to practice self-control and not to murder, God wants you to have a healthy sexual relationship.

The Seventh Commandment is not a prohibition against having sexual relations. It is a safeguard against unhealthy, sinful sexual relationships that will distract you from your relationship with God and that will eventually kill you. Yes, kill you. "But Dad, aren't you over-exaggerating, just a little bit?" No! Unhealthy, sinful, and/or ungodly sexual relationships and experiences will kill you. There is the real threat of sexually transmitted diseases that may kill quickly or may kill slowly. There is also the ever-present reality that unhealthy sex kills your relationship with God and damages your relationship with others, including those with whom you are being intimate. This commandment deals with all forms of sexual immorality. What it says in a nutshell is that all sexual involvement outside of marriage, whether pre-marital or extramarital sex, is a grievous sin against Almighty God. It is an act of disobedience.

The act of sex is usually associated with pleasure, not pain. God created sex. He designed it to be a good thing; however, when we abuse it we are inviting disaster. That is the problem with the popular view of sex: If it feels good, then it must be good; so go ahead and do it. Nothing could be farther from the truth. Do not base your actions upon your feelings. Your feelings can and will mislead you. As a believer in the Lord Jesus, you are called to base your actions upon the truth—God's Word. We will not lie to you; there will be times when your body will urge you to compromise God's Word, to do that which might feel good for the moment. Resist. Do not be tempted to sin, but instead stand firm in God's commandment, "You shall not commit adultery" (Exodus 20:14).

Adultery (having an intimate relationship with someone other than your marriage partner) is much more than a physical act. It is betraying the trust and commitment that is the foundation of a marriage. Adultery hurts everyone involved. It hurts your wife, your children, the one you are committing adultery with, her family, and even you. Proverbs 7:23 warns that adultery can cost you your life. The Ten Commandments are hard, but Jesus was even harder when it comes to adultery. In fact, he declared that desiring in your heart someone who is married, or someone other than your spouse, is adultery whether or not you actually get physically involved. The Seventh Commandment is a call for you to be jealously committed to your wife and to your marriage, just as the Lord is jealously committed to you.

Here are some definite steps you can take to avoid sexual sins. First, guard your mind. The mind, your thoughts, is where sin begins. This is why Jesus would warn against looking upon another woman with lustful thoughts (Matthew 5:28). The act of adultery is not an accident. It is committed with intent. Do not read books, look at pictures, or encourage fantasies that stimulate the wrong desires. Romans 12:1-2 tells us to present ourselves to God as a living sacrifice; transforming ourselves by the daily renewing of our minds. Meditate upon those things that are pleasing to God, "Blessed is the man...who delights in the law of the Lord, and on His law he meditates day and night" (Psalm 1:1-2). Do you recall what Jesus said about the heart and mind? "But the things that come out of the mouth come from the heart, and these make a man 'unclean.' For out of the heart come evil thoughts, murder, adultery, sexual immorality, theft, false testimony, slander. These are what make a man 'unclean'; but eating with unwashed hands does not make him 'unclean'" (Matthew 15:18-20). As the old adage goes, garbage in is garbage out. Boys, you are and you will be the books you read, the music you listen to, the movies and television shows you watch, and the people/friends with which you hang out. Wisely choose the things upon which you meditate and that are renewing your mind. It is those things into which you are being transformed. Remember, you become like the things that you worship. You worship those things that consume your thoughts (upon which you meditate day and night). There are many young men who bow down before the god of sexual immorality; they are addicted to pornography, perversions, and lust. Guard your mind!

The second suggestion is so simple you might be tempted to dismiss it. Do not! Keep away from places and friends that tempt you to sin. Guard your walk. Just stay away; do not go there. If you know that hanging out with a certain friend or going to a certain place might cause you to be tempted, avoid that person; avoid that place. "Flee the evil desires of youth, and pursue righteousness, faith, love and peace, along with those who call on the Lord out of a pure heart" (2 Timothy 2:22); "But you, man of God, flee from all this, and pursue righteousness, godliness, faith, love, endurance and gentleness" (1 Timothy 6:11). There is no shame in simply running away from sin.

Not only should you guard your mind and guard your walk, but you should also guard your witness. Our third and final suggestion in avoiding sexual sin is to think not only of the moment, but rather to focus on the future. Today's thrill may lead to tomorrow's sin. It is one thing to stumble and sin; it is another thing altogether to knowingly and willingly commit a sin against God. Boys, fear the Lord your God, because one day you will have to stand before Him and give an account of what you did and did not do in His name, for His kingdom.

One day you are going to discover what God's perfect plan is for you concerning marriage. If the Lord calls you to serve Him and only Him, then embrace the gift of singleness and remain faithful to Him by maintaining your personal and sexual purity. However, if the Lord calls you to the holy union of marriage, then be faithful to your wife. Marriage vows made before God should be kept in spite of hard times. As a holy union, you and your spouse will have entered into a relationship not only with one another, but with Almighty God as well. Sex is a gift from God and is reserved for marriage only. Any sexually immoral act that betrays those vows, including premarital sex, is considered adultery. The practicality and application of this commandment does not have to wait until you are married; in fact, it demands that you commit yourself to personal purity this very day. When we break the Seventh Commandment, we are sinning against God, our spouse, and against our own bodies. God values faithfulness and sexual purity; God honors obedience.

HOW TO TREAT YOUR CHARACTER

Boys, "You shall not steal" (Deuteronomy 5:19). Did you hear that? The Bible tells us that when you take anything that belongs to someone else or withhold that which rightly belongs to another, you have broken the Eighth Commandment. Theft comes in many forms. When you gossip it robs others of their privacy; it can even destroy their reputation. When you are critical of another person, it takes away their sense of self-worth. When you are angry with another, it steals their joy. Taking what belongs to someone else violates them. It demeans them. Stealing, whether it involves something large or small, reveals a character flaw. It demonstrates a selfish disregard for what belongs to others. Stealing reveals an attitude of self-centeredness, an inclination for satisfying your own desires at the expense of others.

Aslan, Haddon, and Duncan, like so much of God's Word, the commandment to "not steal" just does not warn us away from what not to do, but it directs us towards what we are supposed to do. The Eighth Commandment implicitly instructs us to be obedient to the biblical principle of diligence. Diligence is setting your mind and then your shoulder to the task. It is the

110

hard work of working hard. It is being willing to work hard and to do your best at any job you are given.

The book of Proverbs, a collection of wisdom statements, makes it clear that diligence is a vital part of wise living. You work hard not to become rich, famous, or admired (although those may be by-products), but to serve God with your very best during your life. Take note of the difference between the diligent and the not-so-diligent.

- The diligent become rich and gather their crops early; the lazy sleep during the harvest and are soon poor (Proverbs 10:4-5).
- The diligent make careful plans; the lazy make hasty speculations (Proverbs 21:5).
- The diligent have an easy path (Proverbs 15:19) and the lazy have trouble all through life:
  ◇ They are like those who destroy (Proverbs 18:9).
  ◇ They go hungry (Proverbs 19:15), because they will not feed themselves (Proverbs 19:24).
  ◇ They will not plow in season (Proverbs 20:24).

Boys, please understand us. We are not saying that if you are diligent and work hard, that you can expect everything to be perfect. A proverb is just a generalized truth; there are no guarantees or promises. But, we do know that if you follow the path of the lazy, success and good fortune will be much harder to find. The lazy are also called fools. Do not be a fool. Be diligent and do everything as if you were doing it for and unto the Lord.

Diligence demands that you be a man of integrity. God values productivity, integrity, and generosity. Learn the value of hard work. Your actions should prove your character—prove yourself a man! Be careful that you do not go the way of the fool. There are many ways you can live without integrity: direct theft, fraud, gambling, withholding love, or stealing from God. Integrity expects you to respect other people's possessions. "You shall not steal." Stealing includes taking items that do not belong to you, defaulting on loans, not paying bills, cheating on tests, goofing off at work, cheating on your income taxes, taking sick time when you are not sick, stealing cable services, illegally downloading or copying software, music, movies, or printed material.

Diligence also demands that you be industrious. Ephesians 4:28 calls you to the task of work instead of stealing: "He who has been stealing must steal no longer, but must work, doing something useful with his own hands, that he may have something to share with those in need." Remember, work is not bad. It is good. In fact, it too is a gift from God.

Being diligent allows you to experience the joy of generosity. Not only does Ephesians 4:28 teach you about integrity and industry, it also teaches generosity: "Let him labor...that he may have to give to him that needs." The book of Proverbs also gives practical instruction on the use of money and generosity, although sometimes it is advice we would rather not hear. It is more comfortable to continue in bad and foolish habits than it is to learn how to use money more wisely. Boys, you are commanded:

- To be generous in your giving (Proverbs 11:24-25; 22:9).
- To place other people's needs ahead of personal profit (Proverbs 11:26).
- To be cautious of countersigning for another (Proverbs 17:18; 22:26-27).
- To not accept bribes (Proverbs 17:23).
- To help the poor (Proverbs 19:17; 21:13).
- To store up for the future (Proverbs 21:20).
- To be careful about borrowing (Proverbs 22:7).

Manage your finances in the name of Christ and for the glory of God. Do not take lightly your commitment to the Lord your God. Do not steal from God (Malachi 3:8); give to the Lord what is His (Matthew 22:21); you are commanded to give the tithe (10% of your first-fruits income). Remember, "If you love Me, you will keep My commandments," states Christ. Always give from your first fruits (your first earnings). Give God the best. Give beyond the tithe and give with a generous heart as God has generously blessed you. Give of your finances, your time, your talents, your resources. Give God the best of every area of your life. Do not steal from God.

When you take time to recount the many ways God has blessed you, you will be less inclined to desire things God has given others. Do not be a slave to the debtor. Save money; be like the ant—work hard and save much. Live below your means, so that you can live within your means.

HOW TO TREAT YOUR EXPRESSIONS

The author of Proverbs tells us plainly that God despises all forms of dishonesty. "You shall not lie" (Deuteronomy 5:20). Not only does God hate dishonesty, but dishonesty can actually work against you—others no longer trust you, and you will not even be able to enjoy your dishonest gains. It is wiser to be honest because "a righteous man escapes trouble" (Proverbs 12:13).

What you say, the words that come out of your mouth, have the potential to affect more people than any other action you may take. It is not surprising then, to find that Proverbs gives special attention to words and how they are used. Boys, we want you to have controlled tongues. Having a controlled tongue means that you think before speaking, know when silence is best, and give wise advice. You should also have a caring tongue. Speak truthfully while seeking to encourage. "Do not let any unwholesome talk come out of your mouths, but only what is helpful for building others up according to their needs, that it may benefit those who listen...Get rid of all bitterness, rage and anger, brawling and slander, along with every form of malice" (Ephesians 4:29-31).

Your tongue can be a powerful asset for praise and encouragement, or it can be a massive liability. Take note of what Pastor James has to say about the tongue: "We all stumble in many ways. If anyone is never at fault in what he says, he is a perfect man, able to keep his whole body in check...the tongue also is a fire...it corrupts the whole person...no man can tame the tongue. It is a restless evil, full of deadly poison. With the tongue we praise our Lord and Father, and with it we curse men...can both fresh water and salt water flow from the same spring?" (James 3:1-11). Do not have a conniving tongue—one filled with wrong motives, gossip, slander, and a desire to twist truth. Do not have a careless tongue—one exhibiting speech patterns that are filled with lies, curses, and quick-tempered words that may lead to rebellion and destruction. "Therefore each of you must put off falsehood and speak truthfully to his neighbor, for we are all members of one body" (Ephesians 4:25).

Every time you tell a lie, you are acting like the devil. You need to understand this in no uncertain terms. Lies are not funny, nor are they even clever. They are not "black" or "white." A lie is a lie. A lie is a sin—each and every one of them, no matter how small or how large. As a Christian, when you lie you are dishonoring the very character of God. Do not bear false witness or take an oath to prove your honesty. This dishonors the Lord your God. You are expected to be honest. "Do not swear at all: either by heaven, for it is God's throne; or by the earth, for it is his footstool...simply let your 'Yes' be 'Yes,' and your 'No,' 'No'" (Matthew 5:34-37). What are some of the sins of the tongue for which God holds us liable? You will be held liable for such sins as slander, perjury, spreading rumors, flattery, and insinuations to just name a few. Instead, tame your tongue so that it "comes with love and a spirit of gentleness" (1 Corinthians 4:21).

Proverbs 6:16-19 gives us a very important list of six things that the Lord hates, and seven which are an abomination to Him. Two of the seven abominations God hates deal with breaking the Ninth Commandment: "a lying tongue" and "a false witness that speaks lies." The Bible tells us that God is truth, and as such

He values honesty. Be trustworthy and maintain your integrity by being honest in every thing. Lying can take the form of gossip, false accusations, blame, and self-deceit. It is important to keep promises and be responsible to the commitments that you make. Liars cannot be trusted, and even when a liar does tell the truth, he may not be believed. The Bible warns us against attempting to deceive God.

HOW TO BE CONTENT

Boys, what do you covet? What is it that controls your thoughts? What do you meditate upon constantly? What is it that is your first thought in the morning and your last thought at night? What is it that consumes your mental energy all day long? What do you covet? What have you set your heart upon?

The Bible tells us not to covet. What does that mean? To covet something means to have an unlawful desire for that which is not rightfully yours. When you covet something, you want what someone else has. You long to possess it. Coveting results in jealousy and envy. Jealousy consumes you. That "thing" you desire is all that you can think about. You are consumed with what you do not have instead of being thankful for what you do have. Regardless of how many good things you have, it does not matter because you lack the thing you really want. Coveting is not only a sin; it is not only self-centered; it is a sign of ingratitude to God. Jealousy gives birth to envy, and envy is a waste of time and effort. It turns our focus to what we do not have and away from the things God wants to give us. Covetousness is not limited to money, property, or material items; it could also involve an unhealthy desire for influence, fame, power, position, or even your appearance. Although the Tenth Commandment is stated as a prohibition, it is not a command against lawfully desiring things. It is not necessarily wrong to desire or want things.

The Tenth Commandment is really about trusting God and being content. Do you trust Him? Do you trust that He loves you? Do you trust that He wants what is best for you? Do you trust that He knows what you can handle? The Tenth Commandment is about having a right attitude toward God and the things He has given you. Boys, if you fix this truth firmly in your heart, there will be no need to look jealously over the fence and be envious of what your neighbor has: "You shall not covet your neighbor's wife…" (Deuteronomy 5:21). The other commandments deal with your actions, but this one deals with your attitude—why you do what you do. The others deal with needs, but this one deals with desires. This commandment deals with your heart, because until you have dealt with your heart, the rest of the commandments are only rules we will find impossible to obey.

Do you not know that God values your humility, contentment, and peace? Be content with what you have. Do not long for things that belong to others. Avoid the pursuit of happiness and joy through the accumulation of material wealth, possessions, someone else's spouse, and other's friends. Do not allow earthly things to fill a void that only God can fill. How much money is enough? How big must your house be to satisfy your sense of self-worth? How many cars will you have to own to feel worthy? How many women will you sleep with to make yourself feel like a man? How much more of anything will it take to give your mind rest and your heart peace that you are "all right" with Almighty God? Allow us to go ahead and save you a lot of trouble. *You are not all right with Almighty God!* You have sinned. You have disobeyed. You have been declared guilty. There is nothing that you will ever be able to do to impress the God of the heavens above and the earth below; after all, as far as God is concerned, your good works are like filthy garments. The only thing you can do is trust God, believe in Jesus, and call upon His name as your Lord and Savior. If you trust Him, then ask God to provide what you need. God promises that He will take care of your needs if you seek Him first and not money, popularity, or possessions. Notice what the apostle Paul says about being content in Philippians 4:11-12.

> I rejoice greatly in the Lord that at last you have renewed your concern for me. Indeed, you have been concerned, but you had no opportunity to show it. I am not saying this because I am in need, for I have learned to be content whatever the circumstances. I know what it is to be in need, and I know what it is to have plenty. I have learned the secret of being content in any and every situation, whether well-fed or hungry, whether living in plenty or in want. I can do everything through him who gives me strength.

So the million-dollar question is "How can you guard your mind and heart—your attitude—against coveting?" Here are six practical and pragmatic attitude "shapers" that will help you in guarding your heart against breaking the Tenth Commandment:

1. Give your heart to Christ. Notice we did not say give your mind or give your stuff or give lip-service to Christ. Give Him your heart. Fall in love with Jesus and determine in your heart to follow Him. You will never know true peace and contentment until you have set things right between you and holy God. Accepting Jesus as your Savior and confessing Him as Lord is the only way to reconcile the vast gulf of sin and disobedience that separates you from Him. Trust Him and give Him your heart. Trust Him and follow Him all of your days.

2. Cultivate an attitude of gratitude. Be thankful for everything you have, and as odd as this may sound, be thankful for what you do not have. Give thanks for the big things. Give thanks for the little things. Give thanks for the extraordinary as well as the mundane. You are commanded to give thanks in all things and at all times (2 Thessalonians 1:3; Ephesians 1:16).

3. Learn to love—to love like Christ loves. It is easy to love those that love you. It is easy to love those that are like you. It is easy to love when nothing is expected from you. But we are called to love all people, just as God does (John 3:16). You see, when you are thankful for everything you have and you genuinely love other people,

it is hard to want to possess what they have. It is difficult to be angry with them; to steal from them; to become involved in an adulteress relationship with them; to lie to them or about them; to want what is rightfully theirs. When you love other people, you want what is best for them, not what is best for yourself.

4. Know who you are. We are not talking about having a positive self-attitude or a good self-image. We are talking about knowing who you are in Christ (Ephesians 5:8). When you understand and know who you are in relation to who He is, and when you understand your place in the created order of things, then you can truly begin to understand the basic foundational truth of biblical stewardship: It all belongs to Him (Psalm 50:10). You have just got it on loan for a little while. Having confidence in your standing before God helps you to trust in the sufficiency of God in all things—*all* things.

5. Learn to give. A generous and giving heart is one of the best attitude shapers you can practice. Focus on the needs of others. Be self-sacrificing instead of being selfish. Give to the Lord faithfully, but do not just stop there. Go above and beyond the required tithe; give the offering. Do not give grudgingly, but give with a cheerful spirit and a good heart (2 Corinthians 9:7).

6. The final suggestion we have for you is summarized in the very character of Christ. In 1 Kings, David charges Solomon to prove himself a man by walking in the ways of God and by keeping His laws. In all of history there has only been one man who has ever accomplished this; there has only been one true example of manhood—Jesus, God in flesh. Yes, Jesus was both divine and human; yes, He was perfect in obedience and without sin. But do not forget that He was human. He was a man, in every way that is significant and important (Hebrews 2:17-18). Jesus was (and is) the definition of a man's man—a man of steel and velvet, tough but soft, hard yet compassionate. Boys, be like Jesus. Be steel and velvet, tough but soft, hard yet compassionate. Guard your mind, heart, and attitude by proving yourself to be a man of gentle character.

WHAT GENTLE IS NOT...

Did you know that most (74%) students that are expelled from school are boys? Most felonies (91%), rapes (99.9%), home burglaries (96%), and domestic abuse (92%) are committed by men (Lewis, 1997, p. 46)? Did you know? Proverbs 29:18 states "Where there is no vision, the people perish." The book of Proverbs was written as a father speaking to his son. What vision is being laid out for the young men that make up the statistics noted above? What vision are we, as your fathers, setting out before you?

If you are a father reading this work, what kind of vision are you laying out before your family? Have you ever thought about that? What kind of vision did your dad have for you? What kind of dad did you follow? What kind of legacy are you leaving behind? No matter the age of your son or the predicaments that he has already found himself in, understand this truth: It is not too late, nor too early to define manhood for him. We have started defining manhood for our sons while they are yet young (preteens). However, if you are the father of a teenager and want to start defining manhood for him, understand that there are some things that you are going to have to take back and take away from him in order to restrain your young man. You will need to restrain him and retrain him in how to think and act, but take courage and remember where David was when he gave his charge to his son. David was on his deathbed, an old man. Solomon was a grown man, way past his teenage years. It is never too late to take your role as father seriously!

A TRUTH AS OLD AS TIME

Boys, when we consider the task of raising gentle sons, we think of a story that starts with two brothers who brought separate offerings to God, as was their custom. One brother's offering was accepted and the other's offering was rejected. The acceptance and rejection had nothing to do with the offering itself. One offering represented the best fruits and vegetables the land had to offer, while the other represented the best cuts of meat from the livestock of the field. The difference between the two offerings was found not in what the brothers brought to the Lord, but rather, the difference was found in the attitudes and motivations of the brothers offering sacrifices.

122

Now do not forget, this scene is post-Eden. It is after the fall, after the curse has been laid upon mankind and all of creation. The curse has caused the destruction and ruin of everything, including man's relationship with God, the husband's relationship with his wife, the wife's relationships with her children, and the children's relationships with their parents as well as with one another. This story occurs after "the first family" (Adam and Eve) had been kicked out of the Garden of Eden. Cain and Abel were born outside of Eden to an imperfect father and mother. We want you to learn an important and very valuable lesson from the older of these two brothers. He demonstrates for us how sin can fester and grow within the human heart, eventually becoming uncontrollable. Let us take a quick look at the life story of Cain, Adam and Eve's firstborn son.

After "the Lord God sent Adam out from the garden of Eden, to cultivate the ground from which he was taken" (Genesis 3:23), "he had relations with his wife Eve, she conceived, and gave birth to Cain," and soon after she gave birth to his brother Abel (Genesis 4:1). The Bible tells us that "Abel was a keeper of flocks, but Cain was a tiller of the ground" (Genesis 4:2). Boys, take a careful look at Genesis 4:3-5.

So it came about in the course of time that Cain brought an offering to the Lord of the fruit of the ground. Abel, on his part also brought of the firstlings of his flock and of their fat portions. And the Lord had regard for Abel and his offering, but for Cain and for his offering He had no regard.

Both brothers brought the Lord a sacrifice, an offering of the fruits of their labor. Pay careful attention to that little phrase, "in the course of time." Perhaps another translation would be to state that they brought their offerings before the Lord at an appointed time. Either way, important for us to take note of is that this is not Cain and Abel's first time to go to worship. They had an appointed time to go; they had a routine of going. This was their custom. Undoubtedly, these two had heard all the good ole stories of Eden from their mom and dad—stories of how they had walked and talked with God in the cool of the afternoons; stories of how they had been masters of their environment, working with the land to produce food instead of toiling against the land to produce a crop; stories of how they had once had a close and personal relationship with God. Hebrews 11:4 states that faith comes by hearing, and there is no doubt that Cain and Abel had heard all about the wonderful life that had once been their parents'. There is no doubt that they had faith in what they had heard. There is no doubt that they believed in God.

Although that part of their lives had long since passed, God by His mercy had given this family the opportunity and the ability to keep a semblance of that relationship alive. With thankful hearts they were to come and bring a reasonable sacrifice to God for all that He had provided for them. This was their act of worship. This was their custom. This was an act that the two brothers had probably repeated many times with their parents. But something was wrong with the older son, Cain.

The brothers knew that sacrifices were the method to fill

the void of God in their lives, the void that the curse created. Abel gave a sacrifice out of thanksgiving; God accepted it. Cain gave a sacrifice out of custom; God rejected it. Unlike his parents, who had hidden from God after their act of disobedience, Cain's first reaction to God's rejection of his offering was to throw a temper-tantrum. Instead of accepting God's rebuke through the rejection of his sacrifice, Cain complained and increased the level of his tantrum. He did not show any signs of being repentant.

> So Cain became angry and his countenance fell. Then the Lord said to Cain, "Why are you angry? And why has your countenance fallen? If you do well, will not your countenance be lifted up? If you do not do well, sin is crouching at the door and its desire is for you, but you must master it." (Genesis 4:5-7)

Boys, we want you to pay close attention to a little recognized fact about Cain; he was a churchgoer. Cain was not an atheist. He knew God and he knew God's ways and God's expectations. Cain knew the rules that God had decreed, and he even lived by them, most of the time. But something was wrong with Cain. Cain's wrongness was not found in his coming or absence before God. He was present and accounted for when called upon. His wrongness was not found in his giving; he was a farmer and he gave of his yield. So what was Cain missing? Cain was missing a key ingredient that we hope you will proudly carry throughout your life—a gentle spirit.

Cain was anything but gentle. He was a grouch. This son of Adam never seemed to be pleasant. There does not seem to be one gentle bone in his body. Boys, are you listening? (Dads, do we have your attention?) Such a life, such a countenance, such a witness of character is not good enough for our sons! We want you to know a better way.

In His Sermon on the Mount, Jesus used the word "meek," which may also be translated "gentle." What exactly does gentle mean? It means precisely the same thing that meek does not mean; to be gentle is not to be weak. How can we illustrate this concept for you? Imagine, if you can, a donkey; gentleness or meekness is the picture of a donkey being led wherever its master takes it. If you really stop and think about it, this is a very strange picture. It is strange for a couple of very good reasons. First, donkeys are very strong; they can carry a lot of weight. No matter how hard you pull, or how hard you tug, you are not going to make a donkey go anywhere it does not want to go. Because of its awesome strength, a donkey could really hurt its master if it so desired. Allowing itself to be lead around is a visible illustration of gentleness. Second, donkeys are stubborn. They like to do their own thinking. If that donkey was to set its mind to a task, then it would not be easily moved from that task. So it is very strange to think of a donkey as being gentle and leadable. This is exactly what we expect of our sons. Boys, we want you to be gentle and leadable, not because you are weak; but rather because you are submitted to the Lordship of Christ Jesus, "walking in His ways." We want you to be men of gentle spirits.

Gentle men recognize gentle leaders and they will follow them. Paul wrote in 2 Corinthians 10:1 concerning the gentleness of Christ and refers to His meekness. We want sons who are known to be men under the guidance and leadership of the gentle Jesus: strong yet bold, flexible yet unbreakable, soft yet solid. But there was something wrong with Cain. He did not have a gentle spirit. Cain was the polar opposite of what we expect of our sons. We want their hearts to be right in their relationships between God, man, and sin.

Allow us to say it one more time. There was nothing wrong with the offering that Cain brought to give to the Lord. It was Cain's heart that was wrong. He simply presented a sacrifice to appease God, not to please God! Cain was going through the motions; he just wanted to get back to the fields. He lived by the motto, "Just get me through to next week." The Bible says that God had no regard for Cain's offering. He did not want Cain's offering. He wanted Cain.

Cain felt as though he had been slighted. For some reason, he felt that God owed him one. After all, his family had been kicked out of Eden. Had not God seen the sweat that had poured from Cain's face each day as he faithfully worked the land—plowing, planting, and harvesting? To have God reject his offering must have been truly painful and hurtful. Yet, it was in that moment of hurt that we discover what was truly wrong with Cain and his relationship with God. Boys, if you are not careful, then you too could find yourselves in the very same situation.

Cain thought to himself, in his own heart, *I can live like I want, act like I want—I can even worship the way I want. Nobody, not even God, is going to tell me what to do! Nobody pays my bills but me, so I don't owe anybody anything, especially God. If God wants a sacrifice, I'll throw together a little something for Him, just to keep Him off my back. Why? Because I've got other things to do that are more important; my time is much too precious to take God seriously.* Then the hammer fell. God would not even look in Cain's direction. God ignored Cain; God ignored his offering. This is what it means when the Bible says that God had no regard for Cain or his offering.

When you allow anything to hinder your relationship with God, you allow room for sin to creep into your life. Something was wrong with Cain's relationship with God, and this "something" eventually led to Cain's sin. Notice what the Bible tells you next about Cain's encounter with God. According to Genesis 4:5, Cain's countenance (his face, his expression) fell. In other words, Cain became so angry at God's reaction to his offering that there was an instantaneous change in his demeanor.

His eyebrows grew heavy and furrowed; his mouth drew up and tightened. Cain was mad. Do not forget, this is a description of Cain before he murdered his brother. The problem gripping Cain was not in the deeds of his hands, but rather in the shape of his heart. Cain was mad at God for something that Cain himself had done wrong. God had not approached Cain with a sinful heart. Cain had approached God with an attitude of familiarity that was too ordinary, too common. Cain did not expect to encounter the holiness of God. He just wanted to complete his act of worship. He had made his bed and was now refusing to lie in it. It is as if Cain is crying out, "It's not my fault!"

Let us be clear. The death of Abel had very little to do with the way Cain felt toward his brother. Yes, you can see the steel-eyed look on his face toward his brother, but that is secondary. The death of Abel had everything to do with Cain's attitude toward God. Can you hear Cain whining, "How can you treat me this way, God? I'll show you!" Boys, will you ever think or act in such a way? Oh Lord, we pray not. Will you understand that anything short of direct obedience and submission to God is open rebellion against Him? Yes Lord, we pray that You will teach them to be obedient and to submit.

Cain brought an offering that fooled his parents and his brother. He was the type of person that could fool the people that knew him best, but he could not fool God. God rejected Cain's offering because God knew Cain's heart. Notice the words of the Lord, "Why are you angry? Why has your countenance fell? If you do what is right, then your countenance will be lifted up. Sin is crouching at the door and its desire is for you!" But Cain did not hear God's warning. Instead, Cain only got angrier, so angry that he had to do something. He had to prove that he was all right; that his offering was the better of the two. So in his anger, Cain rose up and slew his brother. That day the world received its first homicide statistic. We do not know if he used a stick, a rock, or if he choked Abel with his own two hands. What is clear is that Cain's evil deed was done because he was not gentle, nor was he leadable. You could argue that Cain's hands did not kill his brother; it was his wicked, evil heart that killed his brother. Cain's heart did not know the meaning of the word gentle. He did not know how to submit his will to God's plan. Cain could not be lead. Sin proved that point.

Cain was wrong in his relationship to both God and man. He did not understand how serious sin was. Boys, one of the things that we love about God is that He never pulls His punches. He never beats around the bush. God always tells it like it is. He always gets to the point and never wastes His words. The text in Genesis 4:6-7 is actually a conversation between God and Cain. Remember, this is before Cain makes one hateful, hurtful action against his brother. We have already said it, but it is worth mentioning again: There was something wrong that was deeply rooted within Cain, and at that moment, his face was showing it.

Take note, God rebukes and attempts to correct Cain. He approaches Cain and speaks to him concerning what is going on inside Cain's heart. *"Cain,"* He pleads, *"Your pride, your harsh spirit, your sinful attitude is eating away at your heart and your relationship with Me; it is quite literally eating you to death! Cain, why are you so down? Why has your face got that evil look on it? You are upset because you did wrong and I called you on it. Do you not know that if you simply do as I tell you that all will be well in your life? Cain, I am going to say something to you that I have never said to another human being. I am going to tell you what is wrong with you; what is wrong with your parents; what is wrong with this land that forces you to war against it just to grow your crops. Cain, the problem is sin, and it is after you. You've got to learn to master it."* Boys, while God is clearly speaking to Cain in this biblical passage, His message is even more relevant today. The problem is sin, and it is after you. It wants you. Boys, we hope and pray that you will never have a conversation like this with God. Learn to master sin!

Did you catch God's explanation as to what had gone wrong? Oh, how creation must have shuttered when God uttered that little three-letter word—sin. God's answer, His revelation explains it all. We tend to think our troubles stem from what is in our checkbooks, or in most cases what is not in our checkbooks. We want to blame our problems on others—our spouses, our parents, our children, our bosses—anyone but us. Most of us believe that if we could just catch a break in life, everything would be different; everything would be all right. If we could just work a little bit harder, then that next promotion would be ours; if we could just get our kids to listen, or if we just had another hour in the day, or if, if, if, if, and the list could go on and on. Your life is meant to be more than just a continuous string of if/then statements. Your problem is not in your checkbook. You cannot blame others; you cannot blame your girlfriend or one day your spouse. Your identity should not be dependent upon your job. It is what you do, it is not who you are. You cannot blame your problem on your parents or grandparents. Your problem is the same problem Cain had. It is sin, and it is after you.

"Okay Dad," we hear you say. "What is it that you want?" Boys, we want sons that have a dynamic understanding of sin and its consequences. We want you to live lives that are the opposite of Cain's. His spirit was restless and his soul was not gentle. He was a tinder box waiting for a spark to set him off. Again we say such a mentality, such a character, is simply not good enough for our sons. By God's good grace, you will have gentle spirits.

How will we take up this fight? How will we strive to ensure that you, our boys, do not turn out to be like Cain? How will we struggle to instill within each of you a gentle spirit that is leadable? We could give you a thousand ways, a multitude of plans, on how we propose to fight for your gentle souls, but to put our plans in the simplest of terms, we will have to mirror the gentle, leadable lifestyle before you. We will have to set the example.

Will our sons see fathers whose hearts are right with God? Will they see us serving God in the local church? Will they see their dads in His Word and His Word in us? Will we have the moral integrity to back-up what we preach with a lifelong witness of action? Will our boys know that their fathers love God with all their hearts, minds, and soul?

Will our sons see fathers whose hearts are gentle toward others? What will they notice concerning our treatment of other people? Will they see dads who are rude and hot-headed or loving? What example are we setting for our boys in how they are to treat their future wives? Much of that depends on how they see us treating their mothers right now. Will they be able to say that their fathers have a good reputation with others?

Will our sons see fathers whose hearts are sickened by sin? Will they know that their dads understand the consequences of every sinful action, no matter how small or how large it might be? Will their fathers live lives that proclaim a zero tolerance for sin, or will their fathers be accepting of a little mischief? Sin has ruined God's perfect creation; both humans and nature itself have experienced the consequences of disobedience. There is only one cure for this condition called sin, and that cure is found in the substitutionary death of Jesus Christ on the cross. His empty tomb is more than a cute story meant to be meditated upon only at Easter. The death of Christ is the only hope that we have for fixing our relationship with God. We desire to leave behind men that are God-followers, men that are marked by their gentleness. Boys, are you ready to accept the challenge? The gauntlets have been thrown down; will you pick them up?

Dads, how about you? Are you ready to accept the challenge of raising God-following and honoring sons who are known for their gentleness? Like it or not, you are leaving behind something: either a son who is clueless about manhood, a daughter who will one day marry him, or a God-fearing, God-honoring, God-following son. What are you leaving behind?

LIFE APPLICATION QUESTIONS:
CHAPTER 4

1) Is there a "Pat's Drug Store" episode in your past? What did you learn from this experience?
2) Of all the Ten Commandments, which do you have the hardest time obeying?
3) Do you have a God-honoring vision for you family? Where do you desire each member of your family to be in their Christian walk five, ten or twenty years from now?

Clay's sons on the beach in Hawaii

HELPFUL HINT

Share with your spouse the need for a Godly vision for your family. Next, devise a game plan that you will use to implement your family vision. Share this vision and game plan with your pastor and other Godly men that can aid and support you as you make this commitment.

END NOTES

Lewis, Robert. 1997. *Raising a Modern-Day Knight*. Wheaton, IL: Tyndale.

Rodgers, Adrian. 1996. *Ten Secrets for a Successful Family*. Wheaton, IL: Crossway Books.

Getting ready for Duncan's first youth hunt

CHAPTER FIVE

Keep His Commandments—God Honors Obedience

O n his deathbed, David, King of Israel, called his son into his bed chamber and challenged him to "grow up" and prove that he was man enough to become the next king of Israel. David's challenge to Solomon was based upon a promise that God had made to him, "If your sons are careful of their way, to walk before Me in truth with all their heart and with all their soul, you shall not lack a man on the throne of Israel" (1 Kings 2:4). If Solomon would be obedient to the Lord and be a man of character, he would "succeed in all that he does and wherever he turns" (1 Kings 2:3). Like any good father, David desired for his son to be successful; but take note, David was very careful to define "success" for Solomon. Success was (and is) all about loving the Lord with all of one's heart, mind, and soul. Solomon was to be completely devoted to God. Solomon's success would be defined by the integrity of his relationship of obedience according to God's standard, not man's standard. Boys, we have one question for you. How will you define success? Will you define it by money, position, power, or prestige, or will you define success by God's standard?

A SNAPSHOT OF SUCCESS

Yeah, we know what you are thinking. "Okay Dad, the correct

answer is by God's standards, but tell me, why are you always so busy going to meetings, conferences, and conventions? Are those things in God's standards?" Ouch! "So tell me Dad, how do you define success?" Such accusations really do cut to the bone; do they not? The plain, simple fact is we spend too much time away from home—hospital visits, new member visits, volunteer recruitments, meetings, conferences, conventions, classes, and the list could go on an on. However, when we think of success, we do not think about attending meetings, work, wealth, houses, cars, toys, position, power, and/or prestige. How do we define success?

Boys, listen to your fathers. We will have been successful in our lives if at the end, when we are on our deathbeds, we can boldly proclaim: (1) we have remained faithful to our God, (2) we have remained faithful to our families, and (3) we have remained faithful to our calling, having faithfully finished the race set before us and having finished it well. It is said that a picture is worth a thousand words. Before we "flesh" these three measures of success out for you, let us take a quick look— a snapshot of what success looks like through the eyes and memory of one of your dads.

Duncan, do you remember those late autumn afternoons when you were seven and we would go deer hunting out on Mr. Sonny's farm? I sure do. Those are some of my fondest memories. Bundled up in warm clothing, we would grab my rifle and our knives, and we would hike back into the old apple orchard, clear out a spot to sit down, and get down to some serious deer hunting. I remember finally getting you quiet and settled down.

You were supposed to be watching the orchard. I was watching the old pond and creek. For the next two hours, every squirrel that scampered across the leaf-littered woods was a herd of deer moving through the farm.

"Shh…," you would alert me. "Over there," pointing toward the noise. "I hear a deer, Dad." After a few moments of intense observation you would whisper with uncontained excitement, "There it is Dad! Get ready." Of course, after a few moments we would decide that it was just a bush, or a shadow, or a branch blowing in the wind. This scene continued to repeat itself over and over again all afternoon.

As the hour grew late and the sun was dipping low over the horizon, I realized that you had not made a noise in at least thirty or forty minutes. I slowly turned my head around to where you were sitting. Remember, we were deer hunting—no sudden movements. We did not want to scare the deer away. What I saw almost made me lose control. I was ready to yell and shout, "What in the world are you doing?"

You were stretched out under the tree, with your hands clasped behind your head, gazing up into the sky. Your little white face was just a-shining. Remember, we were supposed to be watching for deer and keeping our faces and hands hidden. Just as I was ready to chastise you for goofing off, I realized that this was a once-in-a-lifetime chance. There would be many days to be serious about deer hunting, but I might never have another chance to lie back in the woods with you and count planes, or clouds, or the stars. I unloaded my rifle, set it aside, and stretched out with you there in the woods. We spent the next thirty minutes watching all the "stuff" that we could find in the sky. Do you remember that day? I do. *Son, that day was a snapshot of success.*

How does such a day illustrate being successful in life? Success has nothing to do with money or the material stuff that you will collect. It is not about having the largest house on the block or the fastest, sharpest car in the neighborhood. It is not about being the number one salesman in your department or having the big executive desk and brass name plaque. Success is about investing your life in the lives of others. It is about developing life-changing relationships that demonstrate the love of God. That afternoon in the woods was more than a deer hunt. It was a once-in-a-lifetime opportunity to build one of the most important relationships that I will ever have, my relationship with my boy—with you!

Now, I have got to be honest with you. Not all of my choices in life have been so exemplary. I have not always made developing my relationships a priority. I have made the mistake, too many times, of measuring my self-worth as well as the quality of my life by the number of my worldly successes and accomplishments. Each success has been a sweet achievement—an achievement that I have treasured for a moment, but those moments were fleeting. The glory of those successes burned bright, but they burned fast. Before long the excitement, the recognition, and the value of those successes were overshadowed by the next challenge. Like an addict (and I am not one), I was always looking for my next success fix, so that I could have my next success-driven high! Being successful becomes a never-ending marathon of ever increasing challenges and tasks. Success becomes an unattainable fantasy; there is always another challenge, another event, another task. It is the sin of the Tenth Commandment—pride; it is never being content with what the Lord has given you.

THE VANITY OF WORLDLY SUCCESS

Boys, in the final analysis, success, as defined by the world, is a never-ending race that achieves nothing of lasting results. It is what the author of Ecclesiastes proclaims, "Vanity of vanities! All is vanity" (Ecclesiastes 1:2). What does it mean, "Vanity of vanities?" The Old Testament word for vanity better translates to mean "nothing." It is the idea of a mist or a vapor that materializes quickly and dissipates just as quickly. Vanity is the concept of a "something" with no substance, such as the breath of man that materializes and disappears on a cold January morning. Note how the author of Ecclesiastes further defines the futility of all things in life.

- What advantage does man have in all his work which he does under the sun? A generation goes and a generation comes, but the earth remains forever (1:3-4).
- That which has been is that which will be, and that which has been done is that which will be done. So there is nothing new under the sun (1:9).
- I have seen all the works which have been done under the sun, and behold, all is vanity (nothingness) and striving after wind (uselessness). What is crooked cannot be straightened, and what is lacking cannot be counted (1:14-15).

141

- Then I became great and increased more than all who preceded me in Jerusalem...All that my eyes desired I did not refuse them...Thus I considered all my activities which my hands had done and the labor which I had exerted, and behold all was vanity and striving after wind, and there was no profit under the sun (2:9-11).

- The wise man's eyes are in his head, but the fool walks in darkness. And yet I know that one fate befalls them both...there is no lasting remembrance of the wise man as with the fool...all will be forgotten. And how the wise man and the fool alike die (2:14-16).

- Thus I hated all the fruit of my labor for which I had labored under the sun, for I must leave it to the man who will come after me...He will have control over all the fruit of my labor for which I have labored by acting wisely under the sun. This too is vanity (2:18-19).

- He who loves money will not be satisfied with money, nor he who loves abundance with its income (5:10).

- All a man's labor is for his mouth and yet the appetite is not satisfied...this too is futility and a striving after wind (6:7-9).

Tradition credits Solomon, David's son, the same son that we see standing at the foot of his father's deathbed in 1 Kings 2:1, with being the author of Ecclesiastes. King Solomon, himself, is telling us that success, as measured by the world system is "vanity; futility; a striving after the wind." After all, at the end of your life, when all of your wealth, wisdom, fruits of your labor, and accumulated successes are measured and gathered together, who will enjoy them? Not you! "The wise man and the fool alike die" (Ecclesiastes 2:16); someone else will enjoy all that you accomplished. No wonder Solomon states, "Vanity of vanity. All is vanity."

Solomon did rise to his father's challenge. In the early days of his life, he proved himself to be strong. He walked in the ways and paths of the Lord and he followed God's charges, laws, and commandments. When the Lord appeared to him in a dream, "and God said, 'Ask what you wish Me to give you,'" (1 Kings 3:5) Solomon asked for "an understanding heart to judge the people to discern between good and evil" (1 Kings 3:9). Solomon asked for wisdom. Take note of Solomon's own words: "The fear of the Lord is the beginning of knowledge; fools despise wisdom and instruction" (Proverbs 1:7). The Bible as well as tradition tells us that Solomon was the wisest man in all of human history. The Lord heard Solomon's request and honored it. "Behold, I have given you a wise and discerning heart, so that there has been no one like you before you, nor shall one like you arise after you. I have also given you what you have not asked, both riches and honor, so that there will not be any among the kings like you all your days" (1 Kings 3:12-13). Solomon had it all: wisdom, an understanding heart, discernment to judge, riches, wealth, prestige, position, power, and honor. Solomon lacked nothing. You can take him at his word when he states, "What profit is there to the worker from that in which he toils" (Ecclesiastes 3:9); "Vanity of vanities. All is vanity" (Ecclesiastes 1:2).

In fact, according to the wisest man in all of history, there is only one "conclusion when all has been heard—fear God and keep His commandments, because this applies to every person, for God will bring every act to judgment, everything which is hidden, whether it is good or evil" (Ecclesiastes 12:13-14). Why? "Righteous men, wise men, and their deeds are in the hand of God...It is the same for all. There is one fate for the righteous and for the wicked; for the good, for the clean and for the unclean...As the good man is, so is the sinner" (Ecclesiastes 9:1-2). "It is appointed for men to die once and after this comes judgment" (Hebrews 9:27); "For we must all appear before the judgment seat of Christ, so that each one may be recompensed for his deeds in the body, according to what he has done, whether good or bad" (2 Corinthians 5:10).

Do not make the mistake of defining success by the world's standards. You will be judged by God's standard of success. Jesus stated in chapter six of the gospel of Matthew, "Do not store up for yourselves treasures on earth, where moth and rust destroy, and where thieves break in and steal. But store up for yourselves treasures in heaven, where moth and rust do not destroy, and where thieves do not break in and steal. For where your treasure is, there your heart will be also" (6:19-21). What are you storing up? What do you treasure? The old saying, "You can't take it with you," is true. That is what Solomon is trying to communicate in Ecclesiastes. All the effort, labor, sweat, and stress that it takes to accumulate the successes of this life are useless, meaningless, empty, and void when death comes for you. The only successes that have any eternal value are those "things" that you can take with you to heaven. This begs the question, "What is it that goes to heaven?"

The treasures we are supposed to store up in heaven are the relationships we build in the name of Christ. After all, we cannot take our houses, our cars, our bank accounts, our toys, awards, or hobbies to heaven; only people go to heaven—souls. "No man can lay a foundation other than the one which is laid in Jesus Christ" (1 Corinthians 3:11). Lay your foundation upon the mission given to you by Christ. First, love the Lord your God with all of your being. Second, love your family; if the Lord gives you the responsibility of a wife and children, they are your most important priority after your relationship with God. Third, love others even as you love yourself, by "going and making disciples" (Matthew 28:19), because of God's great love for all of mankind. The only successes that can be stored up in heaven are the relationships that you develop in and on the foundation of Jesus Christ: crucified, buried, and resurrected. Any other measure of success is vanity. Be content to follow the Lord's plan for you life.

SUCCESS IS CONTENTMENT IN THE LORD

In His Sermon on the Mount, Jesus defines success for us. Success in life is found in the eternal things of importance, not the temporal pursuits and pleasures of this world. As He concludes this conversation, He makes a summary point and then launches into a discussion about trusting God to provide for you in this life and in the life to come. First, you must get your priorities straight, "No one can serve two masters. Either he will hate the one and love the other, or he will be devoted to the one and despise the other. You cannot serve both God and money" (Matthew 6:24). Once you have your priorities straight, the worries and concerns of this world (What will I eat? What will I wear?) will not consume your daily life. They will not distract you from worshiping, following, and obeying the Lord Almighty. Since you cannot serve two masters, "Do not worry about your life" (Matthew 6:25). Success is found in "seeking first His kingdom and His righteousness, and all these things [earthly needs, not necessarily material wealth and/or gain] will be given to you as well" (Matthew 6:33). Being content implies that you will not worry about what "might" happen, because you have no control over such things. "Do not worry about tomorrow, for tomorrow will worry about itself. Each day has enough trouble of its own" (Matthew 6:34); and "Which of you by worrying can add a single hour to his life's span?" (Luke 12:25). Trust God. "Do not be afraid, for your Father has chosen gladly to give you the kingdom...where your treasure is, there your heart will be also" (Luke 12:32, 34).

If there is one word of advice concerning success that we could give you, it would simply be this: Be content with what the Lord has given you and where the Lord has placed you. Contentment is derived from having a right understanding of your place in your relationship with God. He is God and you are not. He is holy and set apart; you are not. Only He is good; you are not. The only value, the only self-worth, the only self-esteem that you will ever have is found in the person of Jesus Christ and in your confession of Him as your Savior and as the Lord of your life.

Such a right understanding allows you to have spiritual discernment, the ability to tell right from wrong. Discernment enables you to detect evil motives in men and women. With practice it will help you to evaluate courses of action as well as consequences of actions. The author of Hebrews emphasizes that you must train yourself in order to have discretion (Hebrews 5:14).

Only a relationship with God can bring eternal peace. All the "stuff" in the world cannot fill a non-material void and need for a right relationship with the Almighty Creator. Success can not be defined by the number of toys you have. Remember, all that stuff, all those material things that you will collect in your life—they are not yours. They are only on loan to you for a little while. They belong to God. Do not deceive yourself into believing that you are the source of your success: "You may say to yourself, 'My power and the strength of my hands have produced this wealth for me.' But remember the Lord your God, for it is He who gives you the ability to produce wealth" (Deuteronomy 8:17-18); and then again in James 1:16-17, "Do not be deceived, my dear brothers. Every good and perfect gift is from above."

Before we move on to discuss how we hope you will measure success in your life, let us share one other biblical principle with you. It is found in Luke 16:10, and it is a verse of Scripture that you should commit to memory. We would recommend it to you as one of your "minor" life-verses, for the truth of living by it will do you well, and by it you will either experience blessings or curses. "Whoever can be trusted with very little can also be trusted with much, and whoever is dishonest with very little will also be dishonest with much" (Luke 16:10). Be responsible with everything that the Lord gives you. Do everything as if you were doing it unto the Lord; "And whatever you do, whether in word or deed, do it all in the name of the Lord Jesus, giving thanks to God the Father through Him" (Colossians 3:17). Furthermore, do it all to the glory of God; "So whether you eat or drink or whatever you do, do it all for the glory of God" (1 Corinthians 10:31). Wow! What an awesome concept. Everything is to be done as if Jesus Himself had asked it of you—the big things as well as the little things. Do them all well, so that you can be trusted to be given even greater responsibilities (successes) in the kingdom.

What does that mean for you right now? It means that when you study math at school, you are doing it for Jesus and the glory of God. When you rake and bag the leaves in the front yard, you are doing it because God is holy and He is worthy. After dinner, when you scrape your plate into the garbage and clean it, clean it as if Jesus would be using it next. When you go to turn on the television, radio, or computer; when you choose a CD to listen to or a book to read; when you are hanging out at the video arcade, do it all as if Jesus was standing there next to you. Would you want Jesus to watch that program, listen to that music, play that game, read that book, or visit that Web site? As you are doing your chores, do them to the glory of God. Every grade you earn on your report card is a living sacrifice and a testimony as to your relationship with Jesus. When you are driving the family car, cruising around town, remember you are Christ's ambassador. Whether you are at home or church, in private or corporate worship, sing, pray, give, serve, and study for an audience of One.

Lift your voice up as if Jesus was there; do it all for the glory of God! Be faithful in the little things, so that you can be trusted with more—so that you can be successful in life.

This brings us back to that original question: "How will you define success?" As you are being faithful in the little things; as you are doing all things for and to the glory of God; as you are walking and living in the perfect will of God being content with what He has given you and where He has placed you, we want you to define success in terms of the way you live your life. Boys, we want you to be men that are known for their good and generous acts.

SUCCESS IS BEING A GOOD AND GENEROUS MAN

Allow us to change gears here for a minute and talk to all the dads. Dads, we want our sons (and our daughters too) to be good. Yes? That does not sound too hard; that should be easy enough, right? What father does not want their children to grow up to be good? No parent in his or her right mind has ever held their infant child and prayed that their son or daughter would end up on a mug-shot poster in the local post office on the FBI's Most Wanted Criminals list.

We want sons who are known as men that do the right thing in every situation, especially in the most unrighteous and compromising situations. We want sons who are known as men of integrity. While there is nothing wrong with this hope, it is the part of our definition and plan that is going to challenge us as fathers. Raising sons that are "good" is going to give us the most trouble in the years to come. Why? It is not because our boys are necessarily bad; it is simply because to do so is biblically impossible. Confused? Let us explain.

First, as men that take God at His word and who hold a high-view of the Scriptures, God's Word, it is difficult for us to look our sons in the eye and tell them that we want them to grow up to be good men when the Bible clearly teaches that this is an impossibility. Paul reminds the believers at Rome that there are "none who are righteous (good), not even one" (Romans 3:10). In the gospel of Luke (18:1-19), Jesus Himself asked the rich young ruler, "Why do you call Me good when there is no one good except for God?" The truth is that our boys will have moments of goodness and even Godliness, but for most of their lives they will be just like their fathers: imperfect and incapable of doing what is always right all of the time. "The spirit is willing, but the body is weak" (Mark 14:38). This has been man's story since the act of disobedience in the Garden of Eden (Genesis 3:6). The curse has ruined us in every way conceivable. So how will we instruct them to be good when the Bible says that is impossible?

Our dilemma, however, is multi-faceted. There is a second problem that we as biblically conscious fathers must address. As the apostle Paul is closing out his first letter to his "son-in-the-faith," his protégé in the ministry, Timothy, he instructs him to warn those around him who are "rich" in how they are to live. Whoa and woe! This is another huge problem for both of our sons: They are not rich (at least not yet). Their fathers are not rich; their grandparents are not rich; there are no close family members, or for that matter distant family members, that are rich. There is no doubt that Paul is speaking of those Christians in the church at Ephesus who had money. He is not saying that money is bad or that having money is bad. He is simply giving clear instructions to those who have what others do not have—to paraphrase the apostle, "If you have it—give it away." Those instructions are easy enough, but they are not clear enough. How can we tell our sons to be good and generous, when at this point in their lives or perhaps throughout the rest of their lives, they will not be considered rich or wealthy?

Do you see the problem with our definition, our plan? Do you understand why this task of raising good and generous sons will be so difficult? "Boys, be good." *"But the Bible says it's impossible to be good,"* you reply. "Boys, be generous with your wealth and your riches." *"But Dad, what if I am not rich? What do I do?"* For us, it all comes down to how you define the terms. What does it mean to be good, and what does it mean to be rich?

First, we will instill in our sons the fact that goodness is not something that you are. Goodness is something that you do. It is an action, not a state of being. When they help a little old lady across the street, then that is doing something good. If we drop them off at Grandma's house and say to them, "Be good," we are telling them not to give their grandmother "fits." We are telling them not to jump on the beds; not to turn the TV over on their head; not to break anything valuable, and so on. We are telling them what to do while we are away. We want them to be good by doing good things. That is how we are defining goodness. Secondly, we will instill in our sons that riches and wealth are not things that are to be measured by a bank account. Wealth is when you have something, anything, that is valuable to another person, and it is something that they do not have. We want our sons to know that their worth is measured only in who they are, who loves them, and who they represent—not what they own.

Now, how are we going to accomplish that? The world in which we live says that success is measured by one's wealth, his/her riches. And of course, riches and wealth are synonymous with good old-fashioned money—cold hard cash. Relativism is the worldview of our modern society. Being good is all relative to what you think is good. It is relative to your definition of good. What Ted Kennedy or Howard Stern consider good may not be exactly what we consider good. So what are our sons to do? We are certain that Timothy thought these very same thoughts as he read Paul's letter. *But Paul, you do not understand. I am surrounded by men and women who do not think like I do; they do not value the same things that I do. How can I live a good life in such an environment? How am I supposed to be good when nobody else is; how am I supposed to give away my wealth when I have nothing?* Dads, we hope that you can see our problem. What do we tell our sons in the years ahead when they are thinking the same things and asking the same questions? How will we teach them? Our plan is simple. We will instruct our sons according to the Word of God, with a series of questions straight from Paul's very own hand.

Where is your focus?

Instruct those who are rich in this present world not to be conceited or to fix their hope on the uncertainty of riches, but on God, who richly supplies us with all things to enjoy. (1 Timothy 6:17)

Boys, we want you to define the word rich in terms of who you are, not by what you own. We are praying that you will focus on what really matters in life—your relationship with God. If you desire to seek true happiness and true contentment, then you should know that these two things cannot be found outside of God's ways. But that is not enough; you must take the next step.

Paul, in 1 Timothy 6:17, warns that there is the possibility that you might become conceited. When you possess something, anything that others find valuable, it may lead you to become conceited, or high-browed. Paul warns against fixing your hope on the uncertainty of riches. Wealth, that is defined as money, is easily lost, whether it be in the stock market or due to some unforeseen debt, bill, or crisis. We never want your peace and happiness to be wrapped up in riches, whether those riches come in the form of a paycheck or the lottery. Remember, riches fade. Instead, as Paul writes, place your hope and focus your attention on the One who can meet all of your needs, regardless of what those needs may be—physical, mental, or spiritual in nature. We want you to know that when you do place your hope in material goods like money, land, houses, education level, or anything else man-made, you are breaking the Second Commandment. What you are doing is nothing short of idol worship. Idol worshipers trust in their "stuff" and purposefully leave God out in the cold, out of consideration.

Do you know what will keep your focus on God? If you want to stay focused on God, then never forget what the Lord has done for you. The world would have you think that the Lord your God has done very little for you. According to the world's philosophy, all you really need is a little urging, a little nudge every now and again to help you when it comes to your salvation; at the end of the day it really is up to you when it comes to your salvation. That is a lie. It is not true, and it is not good enough for our boys.

We want you to know the truth of the Bible, whether it is popular or not. The Bible does not teach that we are born sick and need a little help, a little urging, or a little nudge. The Bible says that God is the author and finisher of the faith. It says that all have gone astray, like sheep without a shepherd. Without Christ we are dead in our trespasses (sins). We are considered God-haters. If we were simply sick, we could indeed do something to help ourselves. However, we are not simply sick. The only thing that will help a corpse is a resurrection, and dead men and women do not and cannot bring themselves back to life.

Have you ever heard these words sung aloud—"I once was lost but now I am found, was blind but now I see?" Author John Newton once remarked that his little song, "Amazing Grace," was more than a hymn title. He said it was the gospel. We want you to know the truth—that your salvation is not dependent upon some power from within yourselves; "For it is by grace that you have been saved, through faith—and this not from yourselves, it is the gift of God—not by works, so that no one can boast" (Ephesians 2:8-9). John 1:12-13 will be your calling card:

But as many as received Him, to them He gave the right to become children of God, even to those who believe in His name, who were born, not of blood nor of the will of the flesh nor of the will of man, but of God.

All of that, to say this: boys, you cannot save yourself. Salvation is from the Lord. It is an act of God and God alone. That is reason enough to keep your focus on Him.

WHERE IS YOUR FULFILLMENT?

Instruct them to do good, to be rich in good works, to be generous and ready to share. (2 Timothy 6:18)

Boys, it should be enough simply to say that your fulfillment should be found in Christ and Christ alone; if you are going to be good you must be about doing that which is good. Paul instructs Timothy by saying as much. Let me paraphrase Paul's instructions, "If there are those among you that are blessed, tell them to be a blessing to others." Boys, if you are to be rich, then be rich in doing good works. Be generous with what you have and be ready to share it with others. Remember, what you have does not really belong to you; you only have it on loan. If the Lord blesses you with money, spend it wisely. If all you have is time, then share it shrewdly. If you are gifted with skills and/or talents, then use them astutely. Whatever you have, give it away in the name of the Lord. This is the mark of the fulfilled man. He is not greedy; he is content with what the Lord has bestowed upon him. He is not looking for the next best thing.

Be fulfilled and content in whatever you have, even if you have next to nothing. We want to raise sons that are generous. The English word for "distribution" is derived from the original Greek word for generous. Boys, if you have love, then give it away. If you have money, then give it away. If you have wisdom, then give it away. If you have encouragement, then give it away. Most importantly, you are to give away your faith, as often as you can. Share not only your knowledge of the precious Jesus, who died and rose again; but share your testimony, what He has done in your life and therefore what He can do in the lives of others. There can never be a more fulfilling enterprise than doing the work of an evangelist.

WHERE IS YOUR FOUNDATION?

Storing up for themselves the treasure of a good foundation for the future, so that they may take hold of that which is life indeed. (1 Timothy 6:19)

Do these words from Paul to Timothy sound familiar? They should. In the Sermon on the Mount, Jesus (Matthew 6:19-21) said the same thing this way:

Do not store up for yourselves treasures on earth, where moth and rust destroy, and where thieves break in and steal. But store up for yourselves treasures in heaven, where neither moth nor rust destroys, and where thieves do not break in or steal; for where your treasure is, there your heart will be also.

156

When you read the word "foundation" here, do not think of a concrete slab upon which a building sits. Instead, think in terms of a financial trust fund or a foundation in which you invest your money for a later date. Many people have trust funds started for them as children and when they reach a certain age or accomplishment, like college graduation, then the trust fund becomes theirs. Paul's instructions here are clear and they echo the call from Jesus, make sure that your ultimate trust fund is a heavenly one.

Yes, there are bills to pay. Yes, you have to pay your taxes. Yes, if you want a home, car, groceries, lights, and clothing, then you will have to work and work hard. Yes, there is the reality that someday you will need to support your family and be responsible for your retirement. But we want you to "store up for yourselves treasure where moth and rust cannot get to it." Understanding this, there is more to life than clothes or food. Success in life is about being generous and doing that which is good. It is about knowing God and sharing Christ Jesus with others in order that they might also be saved.

As fathers, our prayer is to raise sons who are known for being men who are disciplined, gentle, and generous in their good works. Our task as Godly dads is to invest ourselves in the hearts and minds of our sons. If the Lord tarries and we have the grace of growing old and feeble, we pray that one day you might gather around our deathbeds even as Solomon gathered around his father's. It would be our prayer that you would carry away from us a passion for loving God, a passion for serving God, a passion for living for God. On our deathbed, we would simply remind you of the words of Paul to the Colossian church, "Set your mind on the things above, not on the things that are on the earth" (3:2).

This brings us back to the original question, "How will you define success?" Remember, "The fear of the Lord is the beginning of knowledge, but fools (those who are morally deficient) despise wisdom and discipline" (Proverbs 1:7). Do not walk in the ways of the wicked, "who leave the straight paths to walk in dark ways, who delight in doing wrong and rejoice in the perverseness of evil, whose paths are crooked and who are devious in their ways" (Proverbs 2:13-15). Take note of the psalmist's exhortation, "Blessed is the man who does not walk in the counsel of the wicked" (Psalm 1:1). Your success will be determined by your relationship with God. The successful man is the blessed man of Psalm 1:1, "his delight is in the law of the Lord, and on his law he meditates day and night...whatever he does prospers" (Psalm 1:2-3). As you seek Godly success, we hope and pray that you grow up to be a man of impeccable character; a man of faith who is disciplined in his daily walk before the Lord; a man whose character is gentle and Godly as he seeks to obey the commands and decrees of the Lord—"Love the Lord your God with all your heart, soul, and strength...and your neighbor like yourself" (Matthew 22:37-40); a man filled with the Spirit who is possessed by a generous and giving heart; a man who is consistent in his good works and good deeds—"What good is it, my brothers, if a man claims to have faith but has no deeds?" (James 2:14). Genuine faith in Christ should always result in actions that demonstrate one's faith. In other words, as a Christian, your actions should reflect your faith. The basis of your faith-filled actions ought to be love that is beyond reproach morally. In this way, you will reflect God's goodness to others. Look at what Pastor James has to say about one's faith and one's actions/works:

- "Faith by itself, if it is not accompanied by action, is dead" (James 2:17).
- "Show me your faith without deeds, and I will show you my faith by what I do" (2:18).
- "As the body without the spirit is dead, so faith without deeds is dead" (2:26).

"Listen my son, to your father's instruction and do not forsake your mother's teaching" (Proverbs 1:8). Let us make the pursuit of success as practical and pragmatic as we can for you. As you seek to be this man of faith and action; of goodness and generosity; of gentleness and obedience; of discipline and integrity, we challenge you to define success according to God's holy standard in the three most important relational areas of your life. Boys, you will have been successful in your life if at the end of your life you can boldly proclaim that (1) you have remained faithful to God; (2) you have remained faithful to your family; and (3) you have remained faithful to your calling—that is, having faithfully finished the race set before you—and not just finishing the race, but having finished it well. If you have ears to hear, listen to the admonition of Solomon; hear our echoing cry, "My son, do not forget my teaching, but keep my commands in your heart, for they will prolong your life many years and bring you prosperity" (Proverbs 3:1-2).

REMAINING FAITHFUL TO GOD

The first and the most important relationship that you will ever have is your relationship with the Father (God) through His Son, your Lord and Savior, Christ Jesus, and this relationship is only possible through your lived experience in the power of the Holy Spirit. This relationship must be your priority. It officially started when you accepted Jesus Christ as your personal Lord and Savior. Unofficially, however, it started many years before that. Boys, each of you have been attending church all of your life plus nine months. While you were blessed to be born into a Christian household, neither your mother's nor your father's faith (salvation relationship) was or is enough to "save" you. You are unable to claim the benefits (reconciliation with a holy God; salvation; eternity with Christ, instead of an eternity in hell) of our relationship with God. But that has not stopped us, your parents, from praying for you and your relationship with God.

We cannot even begin to count the number of nights that we have knelt beside your crib, your bed, or that we have stretched out over a desk, or on the living room floor, or even behind the steering wheel as we drove around town praying that you would grow up to be a Godly man, a righteous man—praying for the day that you would realize that you were a sinner (disobedient) in need of a personal relationship with God—the day that you would pray to accept Jesus Christ as both your Lord and Savior. We hope that someday you will experience the indescribable joy of witnessing your own child's decision to follow Jesus and accept His free gift of salvation. Then and only then will you be able to know how we felt when you knelt down, clasped your little hands together and asked Jesus to forgive you and to save you.

Your relationship with God through Jesus was purchased at a high price—the very blood of Jesus Christ Himself. Your salvation was purchased with every lashing, beating, and whipping that Jesus received in your place. Your freedom was purchased at the very expense of God Himself—He who was completely innocent, He who never knew sin, He was made to become sin (2 Corinthians 5:21), so that you could be free. In short, Jesus became everything that you were, so that you could become everything that He is. Boys, because your faith was purchased at such a high price, fervently guard your relationship with God. It is too easy to place your relationship, your faith, in danger.

It seems that in our current day the evening news is more often than not highlighting another story of a pastor, minister, or Christian leader who has been caught in an act of disobedience—an act of sin. Everyday we are bombarded with little innocent deceiving decisions as to whether or not we will remain faithful to our God. Pornographic magazines behind the counter at the gas station attempt to attract and capture our eyes. A sly, insidious remark we overhear attempts to lure our tongues to slander. An innocent conversation that escalates into an angry confrontation ensnares our heart toward hatred. It is so easy to sin. It is so easy to be unfaithful to God. To be a faithful man of God is a most difficult task.

Love the Lord your God with all of your heart, all of your mind, and all of your soul. Make Him your first priority in everything. Remain faithful to Him all the days of your life, for He is faithful to those who are faithful; "To the faithful You show yourself faithful" (Psalm 18:25). "The Lord loves the just and will not forsake His faithful ones" (Psalm 37:28). He is faithful to those who love Him; "All the ways of the Lord are loving and faithful for those who keep the demands of his Covenant" (Psalm 25:10); remember Jesus' words, "If you love Me, you will obey what I command" (John 14:15). Remain faithful to the Lord your God; love Him above all else. This is not only the greatest of commandments, it is the summation of all the commandments.

Boys, to love God is to obey God. To obey God is to deny your selfish desires, not necessarily of just the outward material things, but rather it is to deny yourself of what you are tempted to think, feel, or want that is in opposition to the Word of God. Denial is not to push down one's emotions, but it is to deny one's selfish will. It is the putting of "self" to death. You have heard it said before, "What others do not know won't hurt them"; but the problem is that it hurts you! No! Choose to obey God's Word and live.

> Do not love the world or anything in the world. If anyone loves the world, the love of the Father is not in him. For everything in the world, the cravings of sinful man, the lust of his eyes and the boasting of what he has and does, comes not from the Father but from the world. The world and its desires pass away, but the man who does the will of God lives forever. (1 John 2:15)

Faithfully follow the Lord; "Be strong, and prove yourself a man, observe what the Lord your God requires: walk in His ways, keep His decrees and commands, His laws and requirement, as written in the Law of Moses, so that you may prosper *[be successful]* in all that you do" (1 Kings 2-3). Build your spiritual house on the firm and solid foundation that is the Word of God. "Everyone who hears these words of Mine and acts on them, may be compared to a wise man who built his house on rock. And the rain fell, and the floods came, and the winds blew and slammed against that house; and yet it did not fall, for it had been founded on the rock" (Matthew 7:24-27).

However, you must be careful to "walk in His ways and obey His commandments." You must be careful to listen to His words, for the consequences of not doing so are great. "Everyone who hears these words of Mine and does not act on them, will be like a foolish man who built his house on the sand. The rain fell, and the floods came, and the winds blew and slammed against that house; and it fell—and great was its fall" (Matthew 7:24-27). Do not build your spiritual house on anything but Christ. Boys, one of the scariest passages in the Bible is found in Matthew 7:21-23. It is the passage where Jesus states, "Many will say to Me on that day, 'Lord, Lord, did we not prophecy in Your name, and in Your name cast out demons, and in Your name perform many miracles? And then I will declare to them, 'I never knew you; Depart from Me, you who practice lawlessness'" (Matthew 7:21-23).

These are church people; they are believers (inasmuch that they believe in God, they believe in Jesus). They are good men and women who have done great works for the faith. However, Jesus calls them out. Jesus denounces their works and their false faith. They really thought they were doing it all for Christ, but in reality they were doing all of these works for all the wrong reasons. Oh, how haunting are Jesus' words, "I never knew you; depart from Me." At the end of your days when you stand before Christ Jesus, we implore you do not be found lacking in your spiritual vitality and relationship with Almighty God. Make certain that He knows you. Make certain that you hear the words, "Well done, good and faithful servant! You have been faithful with a few things; I will put you in charge of many things. Enter into the joy of your master" (Matthew 25:21).

Now listen to us very closely. What we are going to share with you next is of a most serious and vital nature. We want you to hear these words. We want you to hide them in your heart. We want you to live by them. Are you ready? Are you listening? Do not measure the intensity or the faithfulness of your relationship with God by comparing your spiritual walk against the spiritual maturity of other believers. In fact, we beg you do not be like the average church-attending believer. We are convinced that many of the good folks that warm the pews of Christ's churches on any given Sunday morning are lost souls who made a half-hearted decision at some point in their life. They have proclaimed Jesus as Savior, but have never professed Him as Lord. If Jesus is not the Lord of your life, He cannot be the Savior of your soul. Many good meaning North American "church folk" have never fully submitted to the sovereignty and lordship of Jesus Christ. Do not measure your relationship with God by their mediocre standard. It is of these people that Jesus remarks, "I know your deeds, that you are neither cold nor hot. I wish you were either one or the other! So, because you are lukewarm—neither hot nor cold—I am about to spit you out of my mouth" (Revelations 3:15-16). God detests apathetic, lukewarm, do-nothing Christians. Do not be one!

Instead, we want you to measure your relationship against the only standard that matters, God's standard. Look at what 1 Peter 1:13-16 says:

> Therefore, prepare your minds for action; be self-controlled; set your hope fully on the grace to be given you when Jesus Christ is revealed. As obedient children, do not conform to the evil desires you had when you lived in ignorance. But just as he who called you is holy, so be holy in all you do; for it is written: "Be holy, because I am holy.

You are called to "be holy." That is a tall order, but that is the standard. The problem we face with following any other standard but God's is that any other standard is inferior. God's standard is best described by being mature in the Word. The Word is best described as God's self-revelation. God has revealed Himself in a number of ways (Hebrews 1:1-2). In the past, He revealed Himself through the prophets, and when the time was right, He revealed Himself in the person of Jesus Christ. Now, in our time, He has chosen to reveal Himself through His written Word—the Bible. We are expected to grow in our relationship with God.

We grow or mature in our relationship as we grow in our under-standing of who God is. The problem, however, is that some-times believers fail to grow. They refuse to mature. "For though by this time you ought to be teachers, you have need again for someone to teach you the elementary principles of God, and you have come to need milk and not solid food" (Hebrews 5:12). The apostle Paul confronts this very issue at Corinth. "I, brethren, could not speak to you as to spiritual men, but as to men of flesh, as to infants in Christ. I gave you milk to drink, not solid food, for you were not yet able to receive it. Indeed, even now you are not yet able, for you are still fleshly" (1 Corinthians 3:1-3). Do not miss out on the "meat," the "solid food," of God's Word, of God's very character. Strive to be different, set apart, holy as you make God your first priority not only in your words, but also in your actions. How can you follow God's standard, be holy, and remain faithful to the Lord your God?

In order to help you place God first in both your words and deeds, we have listed a few practical and pragmatic suggestions for how to accomplish this vital and fundamental task. These suggestions come from our casual observations of those we consider to be true believers; those that seem to be the real deal; those we would consider the genuine article. These indi-viduals have:

- A hunger to share Jesus with others. Boys, you can be different than most "pew-warmers" by simply sharing "the faith which was once for all handed down to the saints" (Jude 3). Do you want to be set apart? Tell others about Jesus. Share your personal testimony; tell them what God has done for you. You have been commanded to "Go, and make disciples" (Matthew 28:19).

- A hunger for God's Word. Study your Bible; "Blessed is the man...who meditates upon the Word of God" (Psalm 1). Get to know the Jesus you are following. Do not just use your Bible as a coaster, treasured family heirloom, a dust-collecting paperweight, or an accessory to your Sunday morning church clothes. Hide the Word in your heart (Psalm 119:11). It will teach you; it will rebuke you (point out your faults); it will convict you; it will correct you, and it will even train you for righteousness (Godly behavior) (2 Timothy 3:16).

- A hunger to pray and praise. Learn to pray. Pray by focusing on who God is; such prayer demands your praise, "O come let us adore Him." Pray by confessing and acknowledging your sins before God, so that you can receive forgiveness and restoration. Pray with thanksgiving, expressing your gratitude to God for His specific acts of grace and mercy. Pray in supplication by making requests, interceding for others, and expressing your desires to God.

- A hunger for community. Be faithful to your church. It is through the local church that God has determined to work. The local church is designed to equip you for ministry (Ephesians 4:11-14); it is the focus of community and fellowship (Hebrews 10:24-25); through your local church you meet the need to worship (Colossians 3:16);

it is through the local church that you have the opportunity to serve (Romans 12:6-8). It has been our experience that those who are genuine believers have a hunger for more than just community; they have a hunger to serve. Be faithful with your gifts, talents, and skills; be obedient to God and serve the church.

- A hunger to follow Jesus. Be an obedient disciple (follower) of Christ Jesus. If God is going to be the priority in your life, then trust Jesus to direct your life. He is Lord (2 Thessalonians 3:16) and has earned the right to direct your life (Philippians 2:8-11). Allow Christ to direct your life in all of its many facets: time (Ephesians 5:15-16); money (1 Corinthians 16:2); abilities (Colossians 3:17); relationships (Matthew 22:34-40); mind (Romans 12:1-2); ambitions (Matthew 6:33); and morality (1 Corinthians 6:19-20). One day, every knee shall bow and every tongue will confess that Jesus is Lord (Philippians 2:10). Make that day *today!*

A NOTE TO DADS

Dads, the most important "thing" you can ever do is to share Jesus Christ and God's plan for salvation with your son (and let us not forget your daughters). It is your honor and privilege to share your faith; it is your duty to share your faith. Hear these hard words. Do not let a pastor, a deacon, a Sunday school teacher, or a friend steal your joy. You be the one who leads your little man to Christ. We know that this can be one of the most daunting challenges that most parents will ever face, but let us assure you it can be one of the most joyful pleasures you will ever experience.

"But Clay, how do I start? Andy, what do I say?" That is the easy part. You do not have to say much. In fact, our advice is simple, "Be strong, show yourself a man, and observe what the Lord your God requires: Walk in His ways, and keep His commands" (1 Kings 2:2-3). That is right; the first thing you need to do is to simply live out your faith in front of your children, in front of your sons. Show them by your example what a Godly and righteous man looks like, what he acts like, how he treats his wife, how he worships, how he works, how he plays, and so on and so on and so on. Next, take advantage of every opportunity you have to talk about God, Jesus, and your faith. Finally, when the time is ripe and your son (daughter) is asking all of the right questions, it is time to share God's plan for salvation. This is accomplished in two parts. First, simply share your personal testimony—how you came to be "saved." Tell your story. The second step is even easier. In fact, you do not have to say a word. Let God's Word do all of the talking.

THE ROMANS ROAD—A SIMPLE PLAN

What is the Romans Road? It is a group of biblical verses found in the New Testament book of Romans that share God's plan of salvation. Dad, go get your Bible and share these Scripture passages with your little man or little woman.

- *For all have sinned and fall short of the glory of God* (Romans 3:23). What does it mean that all have sinned? There is no great mystery here; all means all—everyone.

A simple definition for sin is "disobedience." Everyone has disobeyed the rules and laws that God has established. No one measures up to God's holy standard; all fall short of the glory of God; no one is like God.

- *For the wages of sin is death, but the free gift of God is eternal life in Christ Jesus our Lord* (Romans 6:23). What is a wage? It is a salary; an income; it is what is paid. A wage is something that you earn. In other words, while you are sinning (disobeying) you are earning; you are being compensated; you are working for a payment and that payment is death. Everyone, including you, has sinned; and all that you deserve for your disobedience is death (both physical death as well as spiritual death—eternal separation from Jesus Christ). But notice, "the free gift of God is eternal life"—salvation. Salvation is a gift, and like any true gift, it is given with no strings attached, and it is not given in response to anything that you have done or will ever do. "For it is by grace you have been saved, through faith—and this not from yourselves; it is the gift of God—not by works, so that no one can boast. For we are God's workmanship" (Ephesians 2:8-10).

- *But God demonstrated His own love toward us, in that while we were yet sinners, Christ died for us* (Romans 5:8). This is unbelievable. Do you understand what the Lord has done for you, for us? He demonstrated His love for you; that is, He gave proof of His love with action. At the risk of sounding trite, God "put His money where His

170

mouth was" (John 3:16). God was not caught off-guard by sin; Adam and Eve's disobedience (their sin) did not surprise God nor did it force Him to send Jesus to the cross as a backup plan. The Bible states that "He [Jesus] was chosen before the creation of the world" (1 Peter 1:20); chosen to redeem a people by His precious blood; Jesus was always intended to be God's Christ, the lamb without blemish or defect (1 Peter 1:18-19; 2 Timothy 1:9). God's plan for salvation has always been the death and resurrection of Jesus Christ on the cross. He also demonstrated His love for you by choosing to redeem (save) you before time even began: "From the beginning God chose you to be saved through the sanctifying work of the Spirit and through belief in the truth" (2 Thessalonians 2:13). Also, again in Romans 8:30, "For those God foreknew He also predestined to be conformed to the likeness of His Son... and those He predestined, He also called." Simply put, God predetermined to save you, "He chose us...before the creation of the world to be holy and blameless in His sight. In love He predestined us to be adopted as sons through Jesus Christ" (Ephesians 1:4-5).

• *If you confess with your mouth Jesus is Lord, and believe in your heart that God raised Him from the dead, you shall be saved; for with the heart man believes, resulting in righteousness, and with the mouth he confesses, resulting in salvation* (Romans 10:9-10). After you realize that there is no one who is righteous or holy; that everyone has fallen short of God's standard, including you; that death is your reward for disobeying; that God, however, has set in place a plan to save you from death (spiritual separation—hell), the logical question would be, "How can I receive God's free and predetermined gift of salvation?" How? The apostle Paul tells us that you must confess (to admit, acknowledge, declare, make known) that Jesus is your Lord (master) and believe in your heart (to be totally committed) that Jesus is alive. Belief and confession are the foundations upon which God's Holy Spirit through grace and mercy save you from spiritual death.

• *Whoever will call upon the name of the Lord will be saved* (Romans 10:13). What does it mean, whoever? Just like in Romans 3:23, where *all* meant *all*, well here in Romans 10:13, *whoever* means *whoever!* Neither God nor the gospel is a respecter of persons (Galatians 3:26-29). Anyone who calls upon the Lord's name—everyone who calls upon the name of Christ will be saved. It does not say that they might be saved, or that they could be saved. Paul uses a definitive "being" verb to emphatically state a known and certain outcome. Those who cry out to Jesus with a believing heart and a confessing tongue will be saved.

If you have never accepted Jesus Christ as your personal Savior, we would like to invite you to do so right now. While salvation is free to all who would ask, it is not to be confused with being a cheap commodity. Asking the Lord Jesus Christ to forgive you of your sins is as simple as praying the following prayer of commitment.

Dear Lord Jesus,
I believe You are the Son of God and died to forgive me of my sins. I know I have sinned. I ask You to forgive me. I turn from my sins and I receive You as my Lord and Savior. I thank You for saving me. I want to live for You the rest of my life.

Amen!

What is that, Dad? You have never accepted Christ as your personal Lord and Savior? It is simple if you are ready. If you are going to show yourself a man, to your "little man," then you must walk in His ways. To walk in His ways, you must know Him. If you are ready to "prove yourself a man," then take a few moments to review the Romans Road and then pray the prayer. Go ahead and pray—pray now, just do it; go on.

Yes! What is next, you ask? If you are not already involved in or attending a local church, you need to find a local body of believers, a church, and you need to start attending and growing in your faith. Go get on your computer and connect with a local church's Web site. If you cannot get to a Web site, then use your local telephone book and find a church near you. Ask your neighbor or a co-worker where they go to church and join them. Get in your car, head north, and find a church. Most importantly, make the commitment to have you and your family in church this next Sunday.

Remaining faithful to your family

Boys, can we just "shoot straight" with you? We do not want to belabor the point, but if your relationship with God is not your first priority—if it is not the most important relationship in your life—then the rest of your life will be a complete mess. Speaking of those who reject wisdom, Solomon writes in Proverbs 1:29-32:

> Since they hated knowledge and did not choose to fear the Lord, since they would not accept my advice and spurned my rebuke, they will eat the fruit of their schemes. For the waywardness of the simple will kill them, and the complacency of fools will destroy them.

If it is true that the faithful man "is like a tree planted by streams of water...whose leaf does not whither and whatever he does prospers," (Psalm 1:3) then it is true that the faithless man, the wicked man is "like chaff that the wind blows away" (Psalm 1:4). He "leaves the straight paths to walk in dark ways, who delights in doing wrong, and rejoices in the perverseness of evil, whose paths are crooked and who are devious in their ways" (Proverbs 2:13-15). Heed the very words of Christ, "every household divided against itself will not stand" (Matthew 12:25). You cannot serve two masters. If you want to experience success in all the areas of your life, then you must make God the first and most important relationship in your life.

As you prioritize your life under the lordship of Jesus Christ, He "will make straight your paths" (Proverbs 3:6). Boys, as you prioritize the relationships in your life, God must be first; if you will put Him first in all areas of your life, then the rest of your relationships will all fall in place. They will not always be perfect or even enjoyable. God never promised you or me that our lives would be without trouble, but it is better to be in the house and presence of the Lord than it is to be anywhere else (Psalm 84:10). After your relationship with God, the relationships represented by your family must take priority over everything else. Of course, the first and most important family relationship that you have and are experiencing right now is that of being a son (and a brother); remember the Fifth Commandment: "You shall honor your father and mother." Hear our hearts; you can honor your parents with your life by "keeping our commands" and by keeping God's commands "in your heart."

The second most important family relationship that you must seriously consider will be that of your own family. If it be God's will, then one day you will have the blessing of starting your own family. You will become both husband and father. Now hear us very carefully, we do not want you to be confused about what we are going to say next. Make certain that your decision to start your own family is God's will for your life. If it is His desire for you to be married, then go for it, but if it is not His desire, then remain single and serve God completely. While marriage is honorable, it is not for everyone. Take to heart the words of the apostle Paul, "Now to the unmarried and the widows I say: It is good for them to stay unmarried, as I am. But if they cannot control themselves, they should marry, for it is better to marry than to burn with passion" (1 Corinthians 7:8). Why? Paul goes on to say, "I would like you to be free from concern. An unmarried man is concerned about the Lord's affairs—how he can please the Lord. But a married man is concerned about the affairs of this world—how he can please his wife—and his interests are divided" (1 Corinthians 7:32-34). Boys, make certain that your desire to marry is from God. It is better to be singularly devoted to God, to not be divided in your loyalties. But know this: If the Lord blesses you with a loving wife, the Lord your God expects you to be faithful to her in all your ways. "If you do marry, you have not sinned…But those who marry will face many troubles in this life" (1 Corinthians 7:28). Your success in life will be measured by your faithfulness to God's commands as you remain faithful to your wife.

If at the end of your life you have remained faithful to your family; if you have been a good and faithful son; if you have been a good and faithful husband; if you have been a good and faithful father, then you can say with righteous satisfaction, "I have been successful."

REMAINING FAITHFUL TO YOUR WIFE

Determine to love your wife above and before any other earthly "thing." Boys, there will be times when you will have to put your relationship with your wife first, before any other earthly relationships that you might have (not first before God)—first before your children, even first before your own selfish desires. "You husbands in the same way, live with your wives in an understanding way, as with someone weaker, since she is a woman; and show her honor as a fellow heir of the grace of life, so that your prayers will not be hindered" (1 Peter 3:7).

Remember, when you enter into the marriage contract, you are making a holy covenant not only with your bride, but you are entering into a marriage contract before and with the Lord Almighty as well. Follow His example of love and commitment (John 3:16; Romans 8:1-4). "Husbands, love your wives, just as Christ also loved the church and gave Himself up for her, so that He might sanctify her, having cleansed her by the washing of water with the word...So husbands ought also to love their own wives as their own bodies" (Ephesians 5:25-28). Will you love your wife in such a way? You are to love your wife as Christ Himself loved the church: "Love is patient, kind, not envious, does not boast; it is not proud; not rude, not self-seeking, not easily angered; it keeps no record of wrongs; does not delight in evil; rejoices with truth; it always protects, trusts, hopes, and perseveres. Love never fails" (1 Corinthians 13:4-8). How you determine to love your wife and honor your marriage will govern the quality of your relationship. How will you measure your success in this life? If at the end of it you have remained faithful to your wife and your wife has remained faithful to you, then you can truly say that you have been successful.

Take seriously the words and the instructions of the wedding vows that you might take someday:

Will you have this woman to be your wedded wife, to live together after God's ordinance in the holy estate of matrimony? Will you love her, comfort her, honor, and keep her, in sickness and in health, and forsaking all others, keep yourself only unto her, so long as you both shall live?

Will you commit yourself unto her, for better or for worse, for richer or poorer? Will you love and cherish her and only her, until the very end of your life? Devote yourself completely to your wife. We want you to be jealous for her, even as God is jealous for the affection of His people (Deuteronomy 4:24; 5:9; 6:15). Biblical jealousy practiced in the way God's jealousy is described is not a controlling jealousy; it is not born out of insecurity. It is a description of God's passion for His people, a passion that demands their devotion.

The Lord God Almighty is a "jealous God." He will not tolerate any liaison of His people with other gods. In the Old Testament, God's jealousy—His passion—is a demand upon Israel's devotion. God's passion for Israel is likened unto the marital vow of covenant faithfulness. He leaves no room for misunderstanding. He leaves no gray areas. The sovereign Lord demands complete devotion (Deuteronomy 6:4-5). He is jealous to keep His people holy, even as He is holy. This is how we want you to love your wife, with passion and devotion. You should demand your wife's full and complete devotion, and she should expect nothing less from you.

REMAINING FAITHFUL TO YOUR CHILDREN—
RAISING CHILDREN WHO LOVE GOD

How will you measure success? Remaining faithful to God is one such measure; remaining faithful to your wife is a second measurement of success. But another measure of success will be the ability to look upon your children in your old age, and to see that they have been strong, bold, and courageous; to see that they have proven themselves to be faithful, observing what the Lord their God requires; to see that they are walking in His ways, and keeping His decrees and commands. Boys, make the commitment this day to submit your family to the Lordship of Jesus Christ. Covenant to walk in such a way before your family (your wife and children) that they see what a Godly man looks like; decide this day to raise your children in the teachings of the Lord God Almighty, setting their feet upon the path that leads to righteousness. Hear the words of God's servant Joshua, "But as for me and my household, we will serve the Lord" (Joshua 24:15).

The Bible gives all sorts of advice to fathers about raising their children. "Fathers, do not exasperate (infuriate; frustrate; drive mad; annoy) your children, so that they will not lose heart" (Colossians 3:21). Instead, you are called to encourage (1 Thessalonians 5:11) them and to equip them with the knowledge and understanding of the Lord (Deuteronomy 6:4-9). Furthermore, it states, "Train a child in the way he should go, and when he is old he will not turn from it" (Proverbs 22:6). While a proverb is not a divine promise of what will happen, it is a trustworthy statement of an accepted norm; in other words, if you do "this," then more than likely "this" will be the result you can expect. Children raised in Godly homes, by Godly parents, who are led by Godly men, are more likely to end up loving the Lord with all of their heart, mind, and soul. They are more likely to be Godly children than are children reared in ungodly homes. It kind of makes sense, yes?

How you train your children, how you set the example of Godliness and righteousness, will be demonstrated in the quality of their character. Notice what the Bible says about children, "Even a child is known by his actions, whether his conduct is pure and right" (Proverbs 20:11). Raise children who are wise in the ways of the Lord. Wisdom is good. Set your mind to rear wise children. The man who has wisdom is loving, faithful, and trusts in the Lord. He puts God first and turns away from evil. The wise man knows right from wrong; he listens and learns so that he can do what is right. That is the kind of children you want to rear; that is the kind of men we hope you become—men of wisdom. Perhaps someday we will be able to echo the words of Solomon, "My son, if your heart is wise, then my heart will be glad; my inmost being will rejoice when your lips speak what is right" (Proverbs 23:15-16).

God requires parents to rear their children in a God-centered way. The primary objective must be that your children know, believe in, love, reverence, and serve the Lord. As a parent you must give biblical instruction to your children, not just lay down rules and expectations. Did you know that according to Ephesians 6:4, that the father is primarily responsible for training the children in the ways of God? So "do not embitter your children, or they will become discouraged" (Colossians 3:21). Furthermore, Deuteronomy 6:6-7 calls for fathers to set a Godly example for their children to learn by and to follow. "The righteous man walks in his integrity; His children are blessed after him" (Proverbs 20:7).

We tell you the truth; you will have been a great success in your life, if at its end you can say with all humility that your children are faithfully following God, serving God, and loving God with all of their hearts, minds, and soul. Our prayer is that at the end of our lives we can say these things about you and know that we have been successful.

Remaining Faithful to Your Calling

Success is not about wealth, possessions, power, or prestige; success is about submitting yourself to the Lordship of Jesus Christ and following Him all the days of your life. "If anyone would come after me, he must deny himself and take up his cross and follow me. For whoever wants to save his life will lose it, but whoever loses his life for me and for the gospel will save it. What good is it for a man to gain the whole world, yet forfeit his soul?" (Mark 8:34-38). What is success? Success is remaining faithful to your God, your family, and your calling. You will have been successful in life if you can finish the race that God has set before you and can finish it well. What does it mean to run the race and to finish it well?

Running the race is all about making Matthew 22:37-40 a reality in your life. It is hard to love the Lord with all of your heart, mind, and soul, especially when Jesus defines love as obedience to His commands. Since we do not always obey Him, does that mean we do not love Him? To love Christ is to obey Christ and obedience is much more than lip service. Obedience demands action. You are called to "Let your light shine before men in such a way that they may see your good works, and glorify your Father in Heaven" (Matthew 5:16). Therefore, running the race is all about "walking in His ways, keeping His decrees and commands, His laws and requirements, as written in the Law of Moses"; it is the evidence of "being strong and showing yourself to be a man by observing [all] of what the Lord your God requires of you" (1 Kings 2:2-3). It is a fact, that the proof of loving God with everything you are is by loving others even as you love yourself (Matthew 22:39). Take note of the way the apostle Paul puts it in 1 Corinthians 9:24-27:

> Do you not know that in a race all the runners run, but only one gets the prize? Run in such a way as to get the prize. Everyone who competes in the games goes into strict training. They do it to get a crown that will not last; but we do it to get a crown that will last forever. Therefore I do not run like a man running aimlessly; I do not fight like a man beating the air. No, I beat my body and make it my slave so that after I have preached to others, I myself will not be disqualified for the prize.

Paul is going to run the race of his life, the race of his God-given calling/purpose—not just to finish, but to win! Boys, we know what the world would have you believe; we know what they say in regards to winning. "It's not whether you win or lose; it's how you play the game." To use a euphemism from the King James Version of the Holy Bible, that saying is a big pile of dung (do not be shocked, the word dung is used 28 times in the KJV). It does matter whether you win or lose, and it does matter how you play the game. We always want you to play fair and by the rules. We want you to be men of impeccable character and integrity, doing all things as if you were doing them for Christ and doing all things for the glory of God. So yes, it does matter how you play the game; but, if you are not playing the game to win, then what is the point? Paul runs "to win," and in doing so he disciplines himself for the race. Discipline yourself under the Lordship of Christ so that you "will not be disqualified for the prize"; so that you will know true success; so that you will be a good and generous man!

Generous action, however, calls for regular examination. There is an old management motto that states "You inspect what you expect." In other words, you will pay close attention to those things that really matter (such as your walk before the Lord, or how you run the race). You will inspect them or check-up on them on a regular basis. Notice what the apostle Paul says of his own walk, his own race.

- Paul went to Jerusalem and submitted himself to those who were of reputation (the leaders of the Jerusalem church), "for fear that I was running or had run my race in vain" (Galatians 2:2). Paul not only inspected himself, he allowed others to examine his works and motives.
- "Each one should test his own actions" (Galatians 6:4).
- "Examine yourselves to see whether you are in the faith; test yourselves" (2 Corinthians 13:5).
- To the misled Galatians he would state, "You were running a good race. Who cut in on you and kept you from obeying the truth?" (Galatians 5:7).

Remaining faithful to your calling demands that you have a realistic understanding of where you are on your spiritual journey.

Success is a destination, and you can only reach it if you know and understand from where you start. Always examine and measure your actions against the motivations of your heart. Are you serving, giving, sharing because you love the Lord your God with all of your heart, mind, and soul; or are you doing these things because it is what is expected or because it serves your needs and your plans? Do your actions glorify God or do they draw attention to you? Boys, do all things to and for the glory of God!

FINISH THE RACE SET BEFORE YOU AND FINISH IT WELL

To plagiarize and borrow from the Nike Company, remaining faithful to your calling demands that you "Just do it!" We wish there was some secret formula, but there is not. It is as simple as the little statement: obedience in action. There is no obedience if there is no action. You have just got to do what the Lord requires. You have to do that which you know to be right. You have to obey Him, and if you are going to obey Him with the right heart, mind, and soul motivation, you must do it out of love; "If you love me, keep my commandments" (John 14:15). Paul puts it this way in Ephesians 4:1-3:

> Therefore I implore you to walk in a manner worthy of the calling with which you have been called, with all humility and gentleness, with patience, showing tolerance for one another in love, being diligent to preserve the unity of the Spirit in the bond of peace.

184

Then again in Ephesians 5:1-11:

Be imitators of God, as beloved children; and walk in love…But immorality or any impurity or greed must not even be named among you, as is proper among saints; and there must be no filthiness and silly talk, or coarse jesting, which are not fitting, but rather giving of thanks… Do not participate in the unfruitful deeds of darkness, but instead even expose them…Therefore, be careful how you walk, not as unwise men but as wise, making the most of your time, because the days are evil.

Boys, set your mind on the things of God (Romans 8:5-9). We do not know what specific career the Lord might call you to. We are neither prophets nor the sons of prophets, so we will not even begin to speculate concerning how the Lord might use you to further His kingdom. But this one thing we are certain of— God does have a plan and a purpose for your life. We know that He expects you to be obedient. He expects you to mature, learn, and grow wise in His teachings. You are expected to share the good news of His grace and His salvation with others. The Lord expects you to be His witness, telling the world about the resurrected Christ. He expects you to, "Keep the charge of the Lord your God, to walk in His ways, to keep His commandments, His ordinances, an His testimonies according to what is written in the Law of Moses, that you might succeed in all that you do and wherever you turn" (1 Kings 2:3).

This is how we want you to define success. Do not define your self-value or your self-worth by how much money you have, your position at work, or by the power and prestige that you might exercise in the community. Instead, determine to define your worth, your value, your success by God's standard. Measure your success by the relationships you foster; measure your success by your actions of goodness and generosity; measure your success by your faithfulness to your God, your family, and your calling. Boys...

...finish the race set before you and finish it well!

Life Application Questions:
Chapter 5

1) Have you thoughtfully considered the simple plan listed on pages 87-88?

2) Does your spouse share in your desire to see your son grow to prove himself to be a man of God? If not, start in prayer, and then share the information found on pages 87-88.

3) What type of legacy are you working on leaving behind for the next generation? Does your legacy look like a repeat of your own father's, or perhaps you are beginning a new legacy based on the ways of your heavenly Father?

Helpful Hint

Work with your child to memorize one or more of the verses listed on page 74. Discuss the role of money in the life of your child.

Andy and Duncan deer scouting

CHAPTER SIX

Be Careful of How You Walk

B oys, thus far in this work, we have concluded that we, your dads, desire for you to grow up to be men that display the characteristics of discipline, gentleness, and generosity. These are fine traits that any father would be proud to find in their son. Yet, in our minds there is one more trait that is essential for uniting or tying all of these other traits up into a nice, neat package—faithfulness, or better described as trusting God. If this trait is missing from your lives, then all the others, while useful, will never reach their full life-changing potential.

This particular attribute is rarely ever seen in our day. It is absent from the home, absent from the school, absent from the work place, absent on many tax forms, and even absent in our church houses. Boys, please recall where we started several chapters ago. Do you remember King David on his deathbed challenging his son to show himself to be a man, to heed the teachings of God and obey them to the fullest of his ability? David wanted to leave behind a man who would grow to ultimately trust God in all things. David wanted a son who would take the words of his father to heart and who would run a good race with them; a son who would never stray too far from his father's words of wisdom—words given by a father who had lived a hard life and had come to know that a life lived without God's direction and grace was a life that was not worth living.

Trust God! No matter what life throws at you or where it might take you, trust in God. Boys, it is this simple truth that we desire to bury in your hearts, hoping that you will never stray too far from it. We want you to "stick like glue" to these words. We want you to memorize these words. When you are tempted to leave the teaching of your father, resist. Do not succumb to such temptations, but rather do just the opposite—cleave to the truth. We want you, our sons, to view us as men who trust and follow God. We want you to mimic your fathers and never be known as men who are unfaithful in your commitments to the Lord your God. Boys, in short, we want you to be found faithful.

What does it mean to be faithful? The word "faithful" simply means to be full of faith. It is best explained by the author of Hebrews, "Faith is the assurance of things hoped for, the conviction of things not seen" (Hebrews 11:1). Having faith is trusting that what God says is going to happen will happen, even if you cannot see it happening with your own physical eyes. Faith is the evidence of things that are not seen. How do you know that God is real? By faith. How do you know that your salvation is sure? By faith. How do you know the Bible is true? By faith. How do you know that Jesus is coming back for you? By faith. Andy and I want sons who are known to be full of faith: Sons who cannot be talked out of their beliefs; sons who cannot be tricked into placing their trust in an idol or another god or another philosophy or another worldview or anything other than the Lord their God.

PASSING ON FAITHFULNESS

How do we propose to teach you faithfulness? How can you tell someone to never give up on God, to always take Him at His word? We are going to teach you precisely the same way we teach the members of the churches whom God has placed under our watch-care. Every opportunity God allows, we are going to make a beeline to Scripture and point you toward the examples of Godly, righteous, faithful men who have whole heartedly followed God—men who were faithful to God, even when God asked and expected them to do the impossible.

The author of Hebrews does not leave us with just a definition of faith; he goes on to describe what faith actually does: "For by it (faith) the men of old gained approval" (Hebrews 11:2). This approval does not come from other men, nor does it come from their wives, nor their bosses, nor their government leaders. This approval comes straight from God! What more could a dad ask or desire for his children? Boys, we want you to be workmen approved by God, unashamed (2 Timothy 2:15).

Boys, there is a prime example of a father passing on his faith to his son found in the life-story of Abraham. Scripture is replete with how faith displayed itself in the life of Abraham. Although he was not a perfect man by any stretch of the imagination, Abraham passed his faith on to his son, Isaac, in such a way that it would not soon be forgotten by either father or son. The Bible tells the story of Isaac, who was the son of a promise made by God to his parents, Abraham and Sarah. They were well-advanced in years when God made them this promise, and they were even older when God delivered on His promise.

According to Genesis 12:1-3, God called Abraham to, "Go forth from your country...to the land which I will show you," and Abraham did. God would eventually make a covenant with Abraham, the conditions of which are spelled out in Genesis 17. Abraham was to "walk before [God] blameless," and God would give Abraham and Sarah a son, a people, and a land. All of this occurred when Abraham was one hundred years of age, and Sarah was ninety years old. "My covenant I will establish with Isaac, whom Sarah will bear to you at this season next year," (Genesis 17:21) God promised Abraham. It would be through Isaac that God would bless all of creation. Abraham would have a great name, a great land, and many descendants. What a wonderful promise! Imagine in your old age being told that your line, your name, your family, your heritage would continue on after you are gone. Your children and their children's children would live in a great land that would belong to them, and your name would be remembered for all of history. Surely Abraham reveled in such a thought. The thought, however, would soon turn sour. This promise of a people, a land, and a name all hinged on God's promise of a son—a son who would grow into adulthood and make all of these things possible. This promise was soon challenged, as Abraham was asked by this same promise-making God to do the unthinkable.

Open your Bible to Genesis 22:2 and let us eavesdrop upon God's conversation with His servant Abraham. "Take now your son, your only son, whom you love, Isaac, and go to the land of Moriah, and offer him there as a burnt offering on one of the mountains of which I will tell you." What? What could Abraham have thought about this request? What would Abraham tell Sarah, his wife? How could he explain to Isaac why they were going to the mountain and then what was going to happen once they got to the top of the mountain? We as present-day readers are not privy to Abraham's thoughts or the conversations that he most certainly must have had with his beloved son. The Bible is silent in revealing the precise details of what transpired between God and Abraham, Abraham and Isaac. All we have to go on is what the Bible does tell us. The Scriptures report that Abraham was faithful to carry out God's command. In doing so Abraham demonstrated a faith that is rare, if not non-existent, in our day. Abraham trusted God to do what He said He would do—that is to bless creation through Isaac, giving Abraham's descendants a land, a nation, and a great name.

JUST A CHILDREN'S SONG?

Boys, think about a song you have sung at many a Vacation Bible School. It is a song that deals with the life of Abraham and the promises made to him by God. This song has been sung for many years by children just like you. Do you remember these words—it is okay, sing along: *Father Abraham had many sons and many sons had father Abraham. I am one of them and so are you. So let's just praise the Lord.* Now, you know that you just cannot sing this song. You have got to get into the groove of the song and start swinging your arms, moving your feet, and shaking your head. This is what is called a motion song. If you do not know the motions, this song can be pretty tricky. That is why the simplest way to sing the song and do the motions is by following the leader. Just do what they are doing. Mimic them. If the leader swings his arms, then you swing your arms; if the leader stomps his feet, then you stomp your feet. Just follow the leader!

Our desire is that just like when you mimic the words and actions of this little song, that when it comes to placing your trust and being obedient to God, you would mimic the words and actions of faithful men who have proven to be true sons of Father Abraham and have simply followed the leader. How do we propose that you do this? Instead of swinging an arm or stomping your feet to the lyrics of a children's church song, we challenge you to mimic the actions taken by Abraham during the events described in Genesis 22.

First, Abraham listened to what God said. Scriptures say that God spoke to Abraham and Abraham did what God command-ed. There was no protest recorded. "God tested Abraham and said to him, 'Abraham!' And he said, 'Here I am.' He said, 'Take now your son…and offer him as a burnt offering'…So Abraham rose early…and went to the place of which God had told him" (Genesis 22:1-3). Abraham did not ask God to repeat Himself. He heard the voice of God loud and clear. We want you to hear the voice of God loud and clear; we want sons who hear God's voice the first time. It is not good for God to repeat Himself; oh how we pray that you will never need for God to repeat Himself when He calls out to you. How will we make certain of this? This is going to sound crazy, but we make you this promise. We will raise you to be sheep.

Yep! That is right—sheep. Andy and I want to raise a flock of sheep between the two of us (mind you it is a small flock). Do you realize that in Middle Eastern countries where shepherds still keep watch over their flocks, sheep respond only to the voice that they know? Why? You are going to love this answer. The key here is that the shepherd's voice is familiar to them. They hear it all the time, and all the time they are listening for it. Jesus told His disciples that He was the Good Shepherd. He knows His sheep and His sheep know Him; they know His voice (John 10:14). The voice of their shepherd never leads them astray. His voice never leads them to places they should not go. Boys, we pray that we, your dads, never hear you say, "Well, God never speaks to me." Such a statement will not do. That is not good enough!

Second, not only did Abraham listen to God, but then he acted on what he had heard. After God spoke to Abraham, notice that the Bible does not say that Abraham lollygagged around or that he made a heart-wrenching appeal for a Plan B. The Bible states that God called him to leave his homeland and his family. Next, God told Abraham to trust Him for a son in his old age. Now God told Abraham to take that very son and sacrifice him. At each of these divine points of interaction, all we witness from Abraham is action; he leaves his home in Ur of the Chaldeans and goes to Canaan; he acknowledges the Lord's promises by taking the mark of the covenant—circumcision; he packs his donkey for a short journey, loads wood for the offering, gathers two men and Isaac, and travels to the place God showed him. Abraham was a man of action.

We know what you are thinking. How could Abraham even think about killing his son? Such obedience is preposterous. Kill his son! That is nuts! Yet, somehow, to Abraham, God's plan made perfect sense. Did Abraham know how God was going to reconcile His promise with His command to sacrifice Isaac? The Bible does not say, but it does state that Abraham trusted God and trusted Him to make it alright. After all, Abraham had been trusting God for quite some time: Leave our homes? "Sarah, start packing and call Budget Camel." Going to have a son? "Sarah, break out the vitamins and start knitting something blue." Sacrifice my son? "Isaac, here carry this wood, this fire, and this knife." "Hey Dad, where is the lamb for the sacrifice?" "Don't worry about it," Abraham tells his son, "God will provide `the lamb. Just follow me."

Third, when you read how Abraham listened to God and then acted in obedience to God, please see the underlying current that is being played out. Above all else, Abraham trusted God. The eleventh chapter of Hebrews not only defines and describes faith for you, it also gives you examples of faithful men and women throughout history who have followed God wholeheartedly. Abraham is mentioned in Hebrews 11:8-12 not because of his willingness to obey God's command to offer Isaac as a burnt offering on top of the mountain; Abraham is found faithful for obeying God and following Him to a land where he did not know he was going; for living as an alien in the land of promise; and Sarah as well for bearing the promised son "beyond the proper time of life" (Hebrews 11:11). Furthermore, the author of Hebrews goes on to state "By faith Abraham, when he was tested, offered up Isaac" (11:17). Abraham is recorded as trusting God completely. There is no evidence to the contrary to suggest that Abraham ever doubted God as he was making that long walk up the mountain. In fact, Hebrews 11:19 says, Abraham reasoned in his heart that death was nothing since "God is able to raise the boy back to life." Abraham trusted God. Boys, we want sons who view death as no big deal—sons who understand that for the believer, the faithful follower of Lord Jesus, ultimately life cannot be buried in a tomb; "Why do you seek the living One among the dead?" (Luke 24:5). "For if we believe that Jesus died and rose again, even so God will bring with Him those who have fallen asleep in Jesus" (1 Thessalonians 4:14). Trust God!

FAITH IN ACTION

Abraham trusted God based on his past experiences with Him. God had spoken about a promised land. He found it. God had spoken of a promised son. He had him. Abraham did not understand every how or why of life, but he did know God and that was enough. Boys, the saddest sight our eyes have ever seen is someone trusting in their own goodness or their own success (their stuff or their status) to give meaning and purpose to their lives. The simple truth is that the best we can ever hope to make, or to do, or to accomplish with our hands is a huge mess of things. "For all of us have become like one who is unclean, and all of our righteous deeds are like a filthy garment" (Isaiah 64:6).

We so desperately want to scream at these people—"Trust Him!" There is a huge misunderstanding in the human race that seems to think that God is impressed by our intellect, our talent, our money, our good looks, and our stuff. God, however, has clearly stated over and over again that the only possession that we have that will capture His attention is our hearts. Did you hear that truth? God wants your heart—your total devotion. Place your trust in God. Aslan, we want you to hide *that* word in your heart; Haddon, take *that* word of truth and place it into your mind. Duncan, allow *that* word to transform you into the very image of Christ. God wants your heart!

Boys, listening to, acting on, and trusting in God's guidance is not always easy, but it is required if you are to become the God followers that we envision. Abraham could have questioned or delayed or put up an argument, but no—he faithfully obeyed. His faith was stronger than his doubts. A.W. Pink put it this way, "Abraham's faith triumphed over his natural affections, over reason and over his self-will" (Pink, 1995, p. 196-97). Simply put, Abraham was qualified to raise Isaac as a God-follower because Abraham was himself a God-follower.

Dads, have you been listening? Do you want to raise a God-following son or a daughter that marries one? Are you listening as God speaks? Can you hear Him? Are you acting just precisely as He has asked you to, as He has commanded you to? Are you trusting God, and only God? Is there a large amount of clutter between your heart and His mouth? Maybe you are thinking to yourself, "Well, He has never asked me to do anything as drastic as laying down my son." Could it be that He already knows how you would respond? Hm.

Throughout Scripture we see God acting and moving in grand ways with only those who are capable of recognizing Him.

Elijah hears a still small voice only after a tornado. The disciples see Jesus walking on water only during a storm. Mary and Martha saw their brother come back to life only after they had buried him. The disciples saw the risen Savior only after the nightmare of watching Him die on the cross. Abraham is allowed to hold his son again only after he tied his hands behind his back and had nearly driven the knife into his body. In other words, we want our sons (listen up and pay attention, Aslan, Haddon, Duncan) to understand that their faith will only be rewarded after their faith has been tested and they have been found deserving of such a reward. Whether they are facing temptations, persecutions, or tests, we want our sons to be full of faith. We want them to be faithful!

Boys, what is it that we really want for you? Is it fame, fortune, or health? Would we love to watch you playing sports on television, or hear your latest number one hit on the radio? While each of these or any of these would be good; none of them would be great. No, these goals, these life ambitions are six miles wide and two inches deep (if that), and they are not good enough for you. What about your happiness, what about your safety? Your happiness and your well-being do not matter in the least to us; not one iota. Please do not misunderstand us; it is not that we want you to be miserable, unhappy, unsatisfied, or unsafe. What we do want for you, however, is the one attribute that we know God Himself is going to look for in you—faithfulness.

When the day comes that you meet God face-to-face, guess what He is going to want to see from you? Will He ask you what you did for a living? Will He want to know where you vacationed or where you traveled? Will He want to measure how much stuff you had in this life? Do you think He will want to know how well liked you were? Maybe He will want to see all of your degrees and your diplomas, to see how smart you were? Do you think He will want to know whether or not you could catch or throw better than the other people that He will soon be meeting? Boys, we hope and pray that you have heard the sarcasm of our tongue-in-cheek. What a ridiculous scene, the Creator of the heavens above and the earth below, the Almighty God, wanting to know if you could throw a knuckle ball.

There is only going to be one question that the Master is going to ask of those He calls His own, one thing that He is going to do. "Now after a long time the master of those servants came and settled accounts with them" (Matthew 25:19). When you stand before the Lord of lords and the King of kings, He is going to ask you to give Him an account of what you have done with His stuff (and please remember son, it all belongs to Him—everything). Will you be found faithful or faithless? What account will you be able to give? What words will you hear from the Master's lips? Will it be "Well done, good and faithful servant...enter into the joy of your master" (Matthew 25:21); or will it be "You wicked, lazy servant, you knew that I reap where I did not sow and gather where I scattered no seed...throw out the worthless servant into the outer darkness; in that place there will be weeping and gnashing of teeth" (Matthew 25:24, 30).

Boys, we want you to understand that ultimately the only thing that matters in your life is your faithfulness and obedience to do that which God expects of you. Both Andy and I desire nothing else for our sons than for you to hear those blessed words: "Well done, good and faithful servants...enter into the joy of your master."

LIFE APPLICATION QUESTIONS:
CHAPTER 6

1) List the "Isaacs" in the life of modern men that must be laid down in order to fully obey God.

2) As we tried to do in this chapter, compare your walk with God to that of a sheep and a shepherd. What areas need your attention? In what areas of your life do you hear the voice of the shepherd but have trouble following?

3) Thinking of the life of Abraham, how do you think the following quote could be applied to you life:
   *"When God calls you to a place, He never **meets** you there, He **beats** you there."*

HELPFUL HINT

Assign your child a task you know that he can complete but may not necessarily want to, e.g., pick up toys or take out the trash. Based on his reaction, either whiny or compliant, discuss what true faithful service means.

END NOTES:

Pink, A.W. 1995. *The Sovereignty of God.* Grand Rapids, MI: Baker.

Aslan and Haddon riding the dolphins in Hawaii

CHAPTER seven

A Father's Proverbs

B oys, there is so much more that your dads long to share with you—so many stories, so many little pieces of advice, so many hopes and dreams and desires—but at some point, the conversation has got to come to an end. At some point, you have to square your shoulders, straighten your backs, steel your gaze towards the prize, and begin the journey of proving thyself a man. Boys, it is time. We know that you are still young. We know that you still have many years of childhood ahead of you. We know it seems early, almost premature, to even be having this conversation with you, let alone issuing you such a challenge. But, it is not! It is never too early to start following God. It is time for you to start this journey. It is time for each of you to accept this challenge and to become that man that we have been describing: a man who is disciplined in his character, gentle in his nature, generous with his actions, and faithful in his walk—a real man's man. But before you make that final journey into manhood, let us share a few more tidbits of wisdom with you. As we said earlier, there are so many other things that we desired to share with you, but we just could not fit them all into this book; however, we have picked out a few of the more important and urgent pieces of advice that we want you to remember and to take with you on this wonderful journey that you have started on. Aslan, be the man! Haddon, be the man! Duncan, be the man!

Dads, one of the basic tenets of fathering is to teach your son to accept responsibility for his own actions. Our children may not always listen to what we say, but they are always watching us and imitating us. If we want sons (and daughters) who are good, righteous, and responsible, then we must set the example of what goodness, righteousness, and responsibility look like. Dads, be an example—you be the man!

A PERSONAL NOTE FROM TWO DADS

One of our major motivations in writing out this conversation has been our desire to pass on to you, our sons, the things that we would like for you to know and to live out in your lives. Many of them are deeply theological and philosophical in nature, but some are simply practical and pragmatic—things that we would want you to know and to hear even if we were not here to share them with you. These thoughts are random, and in no particular order. Boys, hear our hearts. We want you to have more than knowledge (the acquiring of facts); we want you to have more than understanding (the interpreting of those facts); we want you to have wisdom (the practical application of those facts in your everyday life). The following is our bulleted short-list of our words of wisdom to you, our beloved sons, in whom we are well pleased.

Courting & Sparking: It's more than simply dating

Son, two of the most difficult sins to resist are pride and sexual immorality (Proverbs 2:16-17). Choose carefully who you spend your time with, whether it be your friends (Proverbs 13:20) or the girls you date.

- What is the difference between "courting" a young lady and dating her? We guess you could argue that it's all semantics (fancy word arguments); however, the real difference is in the attitudes that both of you (you and the young lady) have concerning your respect for one another, each other's families, and most importantly the respect you both have for God, His Word, His Son (your Lord), and His Spirit. Courting is a throwback to an old idea, a concept whose day has passed. It is the commitment you make to never compromise your repu-tation, "your girl's" reputation, as well as God's reputa-tion. There are many aspects involved in the concept of courting, but it is best summed up by the following proposition—The best way to protect your witness (and reputation) in your relationship with someone of the opposite sex is to never be alone with the opposite sex outside of the watchful eye of your parents. We know it sounds old fashioned. It is, and it works!
- Be obedient to the Word of God as you express love in your relationships with those young ladies that you will date, and even someday, your wife
- Keep your eyes accountable (Proverbs 6:17).
- Love demands respect. Boys, always be a gentleman in these relationships.
    ◊ Meet the girl's father.

◊ Ask her father's permission to see/date her;
    and one day for her hand in marriage.
◊ Always go to the door; never sit in your car
    waiting for her to come out (or beeping
    your horn to let her know that you have
    arrived and are waiting for her).
◊ Be the one to open her door and pull her
    chair out.
◊ Remember she is one of God's special
    creations. God values her greatly. Her
    body, her mind, her emotions, her purity,
    and her soul are dear to Him; be certain
    that they are esteemed by you as well.
◊ Find a girl—not any girl, but a girl of the faith.
    Not just a good woman, but rather, a
    righteous woman. As God's Word
    commands us, "Be equally yoked."
    A house divided against itself
    cannot stand.
◊ Be jealous for your girl, not simply jealous.
    Show your passion and never give her a
    reason to look at another.
◊ Treat your girl like the "queen" she is.

On Being a Husband & a Father

- Be home more than you are away.
- Be a passionate and sensitive lover. Keep yourself physically fit and sexually attractive.

- Date your wife and date her often, just as you did before you married her.
  - ◊ Hold her hand in public.
  - ◊ Go shopping with her.
  - ◊ Let her pick the movie or the restaurant.
- Be the best dad you can possibly be.
  - ◊ Get down on your hands and knees more with your children—play with them.
  - ◊ Pray more with them.
  - ◊ Read more to them and with them.
  - ◊ Tell your children you love them more, and always be ready to wrap them up in a big bear hug.
  - ◊ Share Christ with them more (not only salvation, but also share the stories of our faith and describe the nature and the character of our great God).
  - ◊ Talk with them more about anything and everything.
  - ◊ Take them more places, especially the places that they want to go.
  - ◊ Invest more time in their lives than in your own
  - ◊ Let your children see you care for and love. their mother. The kiss they think is gross when they are seven will do more for their stability than you will ever be able to realize.

- Speak more positive words than negative words to your children; you be their greatest cheerleader.
- Live out your love for God in front of them.
- Protect them from physical harm, mental abuse, sexual predators, verbal assaults, negative words. It is up to you to guard their minds and to be their advocate.
  ◊ Know that many of these types of evils can gain free access to your children through your television.
- Do not curse in front of them or behind them.
  ◊ Have righteous lips (Proverbs 10:19-21).
  ◊ Guard your mouth (Proverbs 13:3).
- Let them see you love their mother in how you treat her, how you encourage her, how you talk about her. In everything that you do, let them see you honor her. Make certain that they know you love your wife.
- Read your Bible with them often (daily if you can).
- Pray with them every night.

Concerning Work

- Learn the value of hard work.
  ◊ Always work harder for another than you would work for yourself.
  ◊ Respect other people's property, including their time.
  ◊ Go the extra mile in all that you do.
  ◊ Being on time for a job or a task means being at least fifteen minutes early.

◇ Settle on a profession that you would gladly do for free. That way no matter what your salary, at least you will be doing a job you love.

◇ Work as if Christ was your boss (He is).

- Be careful of how you treat others (Proverbs 6:19).
- Going for that job interview

    ◇ How you dress and present yourself is of great importance.

    ◇ Dress up and dress appropriately.

    ◇ Wear clean, pressed clothes.

    ◇ You can only make a first impression once.

    ◇ Do not slouch; stand up straight.

    ◇ Be the first to extend your hand and be certain to give a firm handshake.

    ◇ Speak clearly and ennunciate each and every word.

    ◇ Say "Yes" instead of yeah, yep, or any other verbal slur.

    ◇ Be polite.

    ◇ Be prepared.

    ◇ Be on time.

    ◇ Remember, a good job and a good salary are not the same things.

Managing Your Finances

- Practice good, sound financial habits:

    ◇ Stay away from credit cards; do not use them,

and if you must, only use them to the extent to which you can pay them off each month.

◊ Make sure you have an emergency fund of at least $1,000; when you are able to put more into this fund, we would recommend having two to three months of income in an emergency fund (no more, no less).

◊ Save for retirement. Start early; the power of doubling your money is much more significant the earlier you start.

◊ Do not purchase more insurance than what you need; do not purchase whole-life insurance, instead purchase term-life insurance and make certain that your family is provided for in the event of your death.

◊ Only borrow money to make major purchases (car and house).

◊ Live within your means. Pay as you go; practice patience.

• Tithe from your first fruits (Proverbs 3:9-10); commit to giving God His portion first. (The tithe is 10% of your income; give it faithfully.)

• After you give the tithe, give yourself 10% of your income; always put at least 10% of your income into savings or into retirement.

- Do not sign for other people's debt (Proverbs 6:1-5); do not make your family liable for someone else's responsibility.
- Do not seek riches, but rather delight in what the Lord gives you (Proverbs 10:4-5); be faithful with a little and store your treasures in heaven.
- Be known as someone who is quick to share with those in need. As you are blessed, be a blessing to others.
- Stay out of debt (Proverbs 22:26-27). The only items you should ever borrow for are your house and your cars. Your house you should pay off as soon as possible (establish a five- to ten-year plan); you should never purchase a car that you cannot pay off within thirty-six months. When you are financially able, you should strive to save enough money to purchase your next vehicle with cash and not go into debt at all.
- You do not always need more (Proverbs 6:18).

Miscellaneous Thoughts

- Be careful to say you love God, if you are unwilling to serve God. "Love the Lord your God with all your heart, soul, and mind" (Matthew 22:37); and, "If you love Me, keep My commandments" (John 14:15). Loving God with all of your heart means obeying God.
- Study the Word of God; be a workman not ashamed, who is approved.
- Spend time in prayer/conversation with God.
- Have a generous and giving heart.

211

- Be an honest man, a man with a controlled tongue. Do not exaggerate. Tell the truth (Proverbs 6:17).
- Have a servant's attitude.
- Do not allow those around you to define you. It is much easier to blend in with the crowd than to stand out. Do not blend in; but rather, be bold and stand out.
- Make choices that glorify God and advance the kingdom of God.
- Set Godly goals for yourself and go after them. This is especially true in your career choices and/or educational endeavors. Never settle for second best in anything.
- True service to God comes out of a true heart of worship.
- Be a man of joy.
- Have a sense of humor.
- Be a man of patience.
- Be a man of commitment.
- Express your love for those who are dear to you. Do not be afraid to show your love and respect for your parents, your friends, your family, and fellow believers. Life is too short. Jesus even commanded us to "love one another."
- Love life and find your God-given purpose in this life. Discover that one thing God desires for you to do in His kingdom.
- Love the lost (the unsaved) and have a heart that breaks for those who are dead in their sins.
- ***Pass these words of wisdom on to your son some day!***

Having fun at a Mississippi State football game

LIFE APPLICATION QUESTIONS:
CHAPTER 7

1) Go over the highlights of this chapter with your son. Are there any that he needs to work on?

2) Are there any additional thoughts, pieces of advice, or fatherly proverbs that you would like to add to this list that specifically speak to your son?

3) Does your family tithe? Why or why not? What does it mean to tithe? Do you encourage the joyful giving of all areas of God's blessings in your life (time, talent, skills, resources, and finances)? Is tithing part of the family vision that you will lay out for your son/family after reading this book?

HELPFUL HINT

Make you own list of thoughts and rules for your son/family. Feel free to borrow from ours. The idea is that you get your "house" in order.

CONCLUSION

He's Been Watching You

B oys, our conversation has come to an end, but we are far from finished. You have heard what is on the hearts of your fathers, and we pray that you have a deeper and better understanding of why we are so serious about the role and responsibility we have as dads. If we could paraphrase the apostle Paul in his second letter to Timothy:

> To Duncan, Aslan, and Haddon, our beloved sons: grace, mercy, and peace from God the Father and Christ Jesus our Lord. We thank God, whom we serve with a clear conscience as we constantly remember each of you in our prayers—night and day...We are mindful of the sincere faith within each of you, which first dwelt in others who faithfully passed it on to your mothers (Debbie and LaNell), and we are certain that it is in you as well. "For this reason...kindle afresh the gift of God which is in you...do not be ashamed of the testimony of our Lord... Guard the treasure which has been entrusted to you."
> (2 Timothy 1:6-14)

If nothing else, know this: Your fathers love you very much, and we only want what is best for each of you. What we are certain of is this: What is best for you is to love the Lord your God with everything you possess. Love Him with all of your heart. Love Him with all of your mind. Love Him with all of your strength. Love God! We want you to chase after Him with every ounce of energy (spiritual and physical) that you can possibly muster and then some. Boys, hear these words, "Be strong, show yourself a man, and observe what the Lord your God requires: Walk in his ways, and keep his decrees and commands, his laws and requirements, as written in the Law of Moses" (1 Kings 2:2-3)!

We were not certain how we wanted to end this written conversation. You have heard from your dads and you know our hearts; but we also wanted you to hear from your moms and to know their hearts as well. Boys, cherish your mothers; cherish the Godly women in your life.

A word from LaNell to Aslan & Haddon
To my dear gifts from God:

First of all, let me begin by saying that I love your dad very much, and I am thankful for the time and effort he has put into this book. He and I long for you to know the things of God. There are many things you will learn in your lifetime, but the most important thing we can share with you is what we have shared with you since the womb, and that is Jesus loves you. I have sung this song to you, and we have learned it together. One of the phrases in that song says, "The Bible tells me so." View every decision you make in life through the lens of Scripture, and by prayer you will make the right choices in life. Jeremiah 29:11 tells us that God has a plan for our good. I pray that you find His plan for

216

Aslan, LaNell, Haddon, and Clay

you. His will may not always be easy, but it will always be the best. I love you!

To be a man is more than just being a certain age, getting married, becoming a dad, or whatever else our culture might say. To be a man, a Godly man, is submitting to God and keeping His commandments. Being a Godly man is something that is very rare, and yet it is that which is most rewarding. God honors those who are obedient and those who trust Him. I pray that your dad and I have done our best to show you what a Godly family looks like. As your mom, I have been blessed to have two Godly men in my life. First, my father was the spiritual leader in my home, and he made sure my mom and I were in church every Sunday. Then I was so blessed to marry someone like my dad who values the things of God and loves me as Christ loves the church. Be those men, boys, and keep our legacy going strong—and please pass them along to my grandchildren one day. I love you!

Aslan, you are a true joy to be around, and I love that we have had so much time together to laugh and learn. Your tender heart and the way you care for people make you such a tremendous person. Haddon, your love for life makes you a person that people enjoy being around. You make everyone you come in contact with laugh, and we cannot imagine a day without your smile and the silly faces you make. You both are the most precious gifts to me, and I take that responsibility seriously. *I love being your mom* and am so thankful that God has enabled me to stay home and raise you. I love you!

Love, Mom

A word from Debbie to Duncan

Dear Duncan,

I praise God for a husband who is willing to dedicate his life to serving God and raising his family in a God-fearing household. Thank you, Andy, for taking time to place what is in your heart onto the pages of this book, so forever your son will know your thoughts. I am blessed beyond compare to be your helpmate. I love you!

Duncan, I pray that you will keep the joy that is so evident in your life at this moment. Do not let anything or anyone take that joy from you. You are a true son of God, and He is your strong fortress, your rock, and your everlasting peace. God is the source of your true joy, please never forget this. When life comes

CLAY ANTHONY & ANDY GOWINS

at you and threatens to rob you of that joy, when your wonderful, contagious smile attempts to escape from your face, turn to your God and allow him to fill you back up with all that He is. Draw all of your strength from him. Do not rely on yourself, the world's pleasures, or ungodly ideas or persons for your strength and joy. God is all that you need. Do as your dad suggests in the pages of this book. Dig deep into the Word of God and obey God's commands. Never take a day that God has given you for granted. Live each day for Him. Look for opportunities to share your faith, to love your neighbor, and by all means to be a Godly example to the world around you. Hide this proverb in your heart, "When I was a son with my father, tender and precious to my mother, he taught me and said: Your heart must hold on to my words. Keep my commands and live" (Proverbs 4:3-4).

Debbie and Duncan reading at bedtime

My prayer for you is that you will take what you learn from your Bible, your father and mother, and those spiritual leaders that God has placed in your life, and grow in wisdom and stature in the Lord. When it is your day to go the way of all the earth and you stand face to face with Jesus, I pray that you will hear these blessed and wonderful words, "Well done, my good and faithful servant. You are a MAN after my own heart!" Duncan, be a man that makes your God and your mom proud. I love both of my men with all of my heart.

Love, Mom

A FINAL WORD TO THE DADS

Dads, we want you to hear a very important and vital truth. Your every action, good or bad, is being observed and mimicked by your son. Do you realize that the kind of man you are is setting the stage for the kind of man your son is becoming? He is watching you!

Our sons are hungry for an example of manhood. They are literally starving. In order to "feed their need" for a manly example to follow, they will follow anything that fills that void. As dads, we can either stick our heads in the sand and ignore this problem—the problem of a lack of manly leadership—or we can accept the challenge of illustrating and demonstrating for our sons what a real man looks like. We can determine to show our boys how a real man loves, acts, behaves, thinks, and serves. If we are going to ask our sons to prove themselves to be men, then we had better set the example by proving ourselves to be men!

220

Duncan and his dog, "Beggar"

Printed in the United States
201975BV00002B/121-366/P